Data Work

A Jargon-Free Guide to Managing Successful Data Teams

By Taylor Rodgers

Acknowledgements

It's often said that it takes a village to raise a child. Apparently that applies to books too. I got through this journey with the help of colleagues, friends, and family.

The biggest thanks goes to my editor Chase Porter. It's not everyday someone who writes a book manages to find an editor who has both the expertise on the book's subject matter and is also a great writer in his own right. For that, I am extremely grateful and recommend him as an editor to any other authors in the analytics space.

The second biggest thanks goes to my lovely and talented girlfriend Alison Burkett. She did the book cover and many of the graphics you see. She also loved and supported me throughout the process and helped me through the many insecurities that goes with writing any book. She's also the most amazing partner you could ask for in life.

Also a big thanks goes out to the talented professionals who took time out of their busy schedule for an interview on this book. That includes Tim Wilson, Nick Stevens, Jared Sloan, Zack Pike, and Doug Washington. Their advice and thoughts on management improved this book immensely.

Last, but not least, special thanks to you, the reader. I hope you enjoy this book as much as I enjoyed writing it. Please share any praise you have on LinkedIn to help support my book and allow me to write more how-to books for the analytics space.

Introduction

In meetings and conferences and trade articles, there are many questions that often come up regarding data. How should you use it? How do you monetize it? How do you find the right people with the right skills to work with it? There's an equally important question though that doesn't get asked enough - *how do you manage the teams that manage the data?*

Answering that question is the intent of this book. I wrote this for business executives and managers who find themselves in a new role overseeing data professionals. More specifically, I wrote this book for executives who have little experience in business intelligence or data science.

Why would I make this my book's target audience?

Because great work in business intelligence comes from **great operations** – not from individual performance. You can hire the best employees and still fail with your data initiatives if you don't operate effectively.

And who has the biggest impact on operations? **Management.**

In fact, I'd argue a great manager will do better with a team of average developers than a mediocre manager with a team of phenomenal developers.

The problem is that many who find themselves overseeing data teams have little to no experience in data. They were chosen for their soft skills, their ability to think strategically, and their vision.

This book won't tell you what vision you should have. That's not my place. I can't advise you on the soft skills part either. I think that's contextual and often a matter of opinion. And I can't guide your strategy. That's entirely based on the needs of the stakeholder.

I can help you with the operations part though, at least where it matters most to the success of data solutions.

Building a Better Business Ecosystem

If there's a big theme to this book, it is that you're improving the **business ecosystem**, not just building a data team. That's a more grandiose way of saying you're just improving operations, but it's the best way to describe my advice. Your goal is to improve the environment your team works in so they naturally produce better results.

Most management books focus on using your personality and soft skills to improve results. This book however focuses on practical actions you can take to improve operations. That's because data, by its very nature, requires operational efficiency.

By focusing on operations, your stakeholders will be more satisfied. Your team's work will be more timely, accessible, relevant, and accurate. Your individual contributors will have an easier time delivering these results – and they'll actually like their jobs too.

So what goes into building a better ecosystem? To answer this, we'll explore the following topics:
1. What makes a successful data solution?
2. How do operations impact data quality?
3. What processes improve output and stakeholder satisfaction?
4. How do you manage stakeholders and their expectations?
5. What tools or software improve your data solutions?
6. What types of roles improve your data solutions?
7. How to hire, manage, and retain data professionals?

This book will answer all of these questions and clearly lay out a path to success in building data teams and producing data work.

A Few Notes About This Book

Before moving forward, I want to make a few notes about this book.

This book is an operational handbook. The advice is based on my own experiences, research on operational improvement, and interviews with managers and executives with relevant expertise. Some things may not apply to your organization. That's fine. Use what you find useful and discard what you don't.

But if you don't know where else to begin, this book is a good template to get started until you feel confident creating your own methods.

My advice applies to anyone that touches data – regardless of title. For that reason, I often refer to data professionals (BI developers, data scientists, data analysts, database developers) as **data workers.** While each role has unique challenges for managers, there are enough similarities for my advice to apply to most employees, most of the time.

In addition, I also use the term **data work** to include *data science, business intelligence, data and analytics,* and the broader *data profession.*

If you want to get really specific, this book deals more with the business intelligence side of things, which means automating and improving the data collection and reporting process. That does *not* mean my book does not serve your goals for pursuing data science, machine learning, and predictive analytics. Far from it. Following my advice, you'll achieve operational maturity far sooner and transition more seamlessly towards advanced analytics.

With that out of the way, I hope you find this book as valuable as I intend. Let's begin!

1

What Is Success for a Data Team Manager?

If your company wants to invest in data, they probably have a problem to solve. The solution to that problem could be report automation and reducing reliance on Excel spreadsheets. Or it could be a data warehouse. Maybe even predictive analytics. The possibilities are endless.

Many people say delivering that solution is how the manager succeeds. I disagree. Those solutions are how your **stakeholders** and the **company** define success. The way a **manager** achieves that success is different.

A manager builds and improves operations so that his or her team can build those solutions themselves. The quality of your team's output will improve or diminish over time based on how well the operations perform. The person with the best view of operations and the power to influence it is the manager.

Project-based Outcomes versus Continuous Outcomes

Let's say you and your spouse recently bought a fixer-upper home. You have big plans to improve the property and make it the best one in the neighborhood.

You immediately start on the landscaping, which is the first of many major renovations. You remove the weeds and overgrown shrubs. You plant new trees and flower beds. You replace the fence, add a pond, and even build a new patio.

After a few weekends of hard work, you're done. Friends, family, and neighbors all have nice things to say about your new and improved garden.

But then things change. You start work on your next major renovation, which is the kitchen. You and your spouse spend the next few months gutting the kitchen, installing new cabinets, adding a new stove, new sink, etc. You tile, spackle, paint, and so on and so on.

The garden, however, starts to be neglected. Weeds and volunteer trees grow in places you don't want them. You don't have time to rake either, which means your entire yard is covered in leaves, smothering both your yard and flower bed.

By the time you finish your kitchen, the landscape surrounding the house has decayed and is no longer the "gem of the neighborhood."

Pick up on the theme I'm making?

Building the garden is a **project-based outcome**. You and your spouse wanted something beautiful in the short-term and you got it. The problem is you didn't focus on long-term maintenance, which is a **continuous outcome**. All your hard work went out the door because you didn't pull weeds, take out volunteer trees, and rake the leaves.

It's easy for managers to get carried away with focusing on project-based outcomes. Those are generally sexier and make it look like the managers are accomplishing a lot. At trade conferences, people who oversee data teams often talk about how they delivered such-and-such solution with such-and-such strategy.

That's all well and good, but often behind every big speech announcing how great a data solution went, there are several people who are beyond frustrated with it. The solution probably worked fine in the beginning, but the data doesn't answer the questions that stakeholders thought it would. The data that does come through is often wrong. People who support the solution don't do what they're supposed to do, either because of their incompetence or ignorance (usually ignorance).

In shorter words, the manager neglected the garden in an attempt to finish the new kitchen.

If you want to build something that works in the long-run, change your focus from delivering project-based outcomes to continuous outcomes. Your team members should build projects based on the requirements they gather. Your job is to build an operation and a culture that makes sure those solutions continue to work.

The sad irony is that success with continuous outcomes is far less visible than failure, but failure with continuous outcomes will eventually get you fired. Data quality will diminish, your reporting and analysis will be useless, and whatever charm you had with stakeholders won't save you.

Success in continuous outcomes also means saying no to short-term solutions and decisions. Sometimes this will make stakeholders and your own employees very frustrated. Short-term solutions are often hacks that don't scale well and ruin quality as you grow your operations.

You can change this by focusing your team on delivering the project-based outcomes in the short term, while you build an operation to achieve the continuous outcomes your company needs in the long term. Your stakeholders may never notice that you succeed at this, but they will certainly notice if you fail. With hard work and the right focus however, you can be the person who builds the garden and actually maintains it as well.

What Makes a Successful Data Solution?

Success starts with stakeholders who want data. They have a hierarchy of needs you must fulfill to make them happy. I developed *Taylor Rodgers' Pyramid of Data Solution Success* to illustrate those needs. If you meet all of them, you'll make your stakeholders happy. And happy stakeholders means a happy life.

Data Quality and Accuracy

Data quality and accuracy is the foundation of success and it's something people new to data neglect at their peril. You as a manager should not neglect it. Data quality issues can become rampant as your operation scales. If it becomes obvious that your data is inaccurate, stakeholders will stop trusting it, stop using it, and organizational support for your solutions will die.

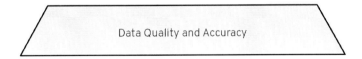

Operations impact data quality more than anything else on this pyramid. And the person who impacts operations the most is the manager. For that reason, I'll devote a whole chapter to data quality and the ways to improve it.

Data Relevancy

Data relevancy means your team's data is actually useful to stakeholders. For example, a social media manager is less interested in how many people visited her client's website as how many people interacted with their Facebook posts.

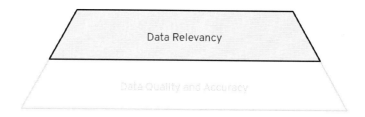

The best way to ensure data relevancy is thorough requirements gathering. Your team is primarily responsible for gathering requirements, but your job is supporting them in that process. I devote an entire chapter to requirements gathering and another chapter on how to handle stakeholders involved in these discussions.

Reporting and Analysis Readability

Reporting and analysis readability relates to how you translate data for your stakeholders, including aesthetics and presentation methods. Your team's skill at designing dashboards and presenting analyses affects how easily stakeholders can digest this information.

This is more dependent on individual skill level than it is on the operations. I do not provide a chapter on this, but there are various resources out there on communicating data through writing, dashboard design, and public speaking.

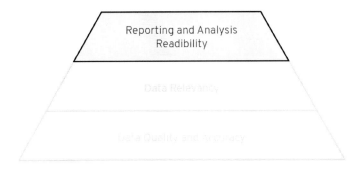

Timely Delivery

Timely delivery is how quickly data solutions are turned around and how frequently the data updates. Database developers have the biggest impact here. They automate the extraction of data from one system to another where report developers and analysts can access it.

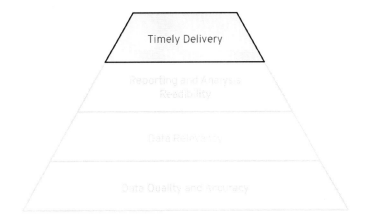

Positive Stakeholder Experience

Positive stakeholder experience depends on your team's soft skills and the process a stakeholder must follow to get data solutions created. If you make the process transparent, explain it well, and your team is polite in their interactions, the stakeholder will be happier.

But the great irony is that you cannot make up for failure at the bottom of the pyramid with excellence at the top. People would rather have accurate and relevant data in an Excel spreadsheet than a beautiful Tableau report that's wrong. If you were someone that could deliver accurate, relevant, and engaging dashboards in a timely manner, but had a loathsome personality, you'd still be more successful than someone who was extremely likeable, but failed at any of the lower levels on the pyramid.

You Approach This Pyramid Differently Than Your Team

The big difference between you and your team is how you approach this pyramid. Your team will fulfill these needs by the way they approach projects. You fulfill it by the way you approach operations.

Another way to put that: one is **project-based** and the other is **continuous-based**.

Things to Remember

- Project-based outcomes are how your stakeholders and team define success
- Continuous outcomes is what defines success for a manager
- Successful data solutions must fulfill the following needs in the order they appear:
    - Data quality
    - Reporting and analysis relevancy
    - Reporting and analysis readability
    - Timely delivery
    - Positive stakeholder experience
- Both project-based and continuous outcomes should fulfill those needs, but the approach is different for each

2

Why Data Quality Issues Happen and What You Can Do About It

"If you show someone something and they figure out that it's wrong – everything is wrong." – Zack Pike, VP of Data Strategy at Callahan

As you recall from the *Pyramid of Data Solution Success,* the foundation of everything we do is data and report quality. When your data, reports, and analysis are consistently inaccurate, and the stakeholder notices, they will not care what else you can deliver.

Data quality is seldom a reflection of one individual team member. It's a reflection of the health of an organization. Data quality issues usually stem from data **flow** issues. If data cannot efficiently move from point A to point B, then there is likely a communication breakdown, process breakdown, or technological breakdown. All of those things are operational issues.

And that means **you** the manager are ultimately responsible for ensuring data quality.

I'm not exaggerating. If someone hired me to measure the success of a BI manager, the first thing I would do is measure data quality. I've done many data quality analyses and audits, and the root cause of those issues always stemmed from operational failure.

As a matter of fact, when I first started writing this book, the title was going to be *How to Identify and Fix Data Quality Issues.*

But I found that the solutions to these problems almost always pointed back to management and the operations they put in place. They would need to improve processes, provide better training, establish better communication, or reassign responsibilities.

If those managers did that on a continuous basis, it would eliminate the need to identify quality issues most of the time.

Personality Won't Save You and Can't Save Your Employees

We all know that story of a brilliant jerk who got fired because of an insufferable personality. We view that as a lesson that people prefer to work with likable people over just talent. Everyone wants to work with highly conscientious people, but there's a limit when it comes to data quality.

"The number one thing that everyone cares about is the confidence in the data," said Nick Stevens, the Chief Data Officer of the University of Kansas. "Depending on your personality type, you either get away with it zero times or ten times. But at some point, you're gonna reach the threshold."

Data Quality Issues Are More Widespread Than You Think

The odds of delivering a perfect data solution on a systematic and continuous level are literally stacked against you. To illustrate this, look at the chart on the next page.

This chart shows how a process or workflow has less success the more steps you have. If you have a process with 200 independent steps and all succeed 99% of the time, the probability of all 200 succeeding is approximately 13%.

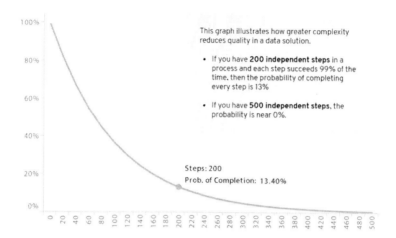

Probability of Success

This graph illustrates how greater complexity reduces quality in a data solution.

- If you have **200 independent steps** in a process and each step succeeds 99% of the time, then the probability of completing every step is 13%

- If you have **500 independent steps**, the probability is near 0%.

Steps: 200
Prob. of Completion: 13.40%

Graff, R. (2017, December 13). A short equation explains why simplicity is the best policy. Retrieved March 07, 2021, from https://qz.com/work/1154701/a-short-equation-explains-why-simplicity-is-the-best-policy/

The process of extracting, manipulating, uploading, reporting, and analyzing data requires thousands of steps and multiple teams working together. With all those moving parts and dependencies, it's extremely easy for data quality to decline.

Every time I've evaluated data quality and presented my findings to leadership, they are always surprised at how bad it really is. The more you work with data over time however, the less surprised you become.

What Are Common Reasons for Data Quality Issues?

Data quality issues typically resort from the following:
- Operation scaling
- Lack of training / communication
- Frequent process changes / reorganization

- Tight deadlines
- Poor understanding of the data
- Employee inexperience
- Employee error
- Employee incompetence
- High employee turnover
- Disinterest of management

You'll likely notice that nearly all of those are impacted by management. Employee inexperience is the only one you can't control (outside of hiring only experienced professionals), but you (the manager) can impact the rest directly.

Data Quality Issues Caused By Operational Scaling

Operation scaling hurts data quality. For example, think of a company that builds websites for clients. They often include other marketing services as well, such as social media management and digital media buying.

If the company builds one website per quarter and has five specialized employees (web developer, BI developer, social media manager, paid media buyer, and copywriter), then communication is simple. If someone forgot to tell the BI developer of a website change, it isn't a big hassle to retrofit tracking.

That changes when the company builds a new website every week and has whole departments managing different components of the marketing strategy. If a strong manager is not overseeing and building standards, the project can easily go haywire.

For example, the social media manager buying ads on Facebook and writing organic posts may not know to set up unique Google Analytics UTM parameters for each specific campaign.

The paid media buyer may abruptly change the way they use Google Ads without consulting the data team. For example, he may have previously used a single Google Ads account per client website. He then decides to make it easier on himself by creating one account for all client websites. That makes his job easier but effectively breaks how Google Ads data is mapped to other tools.

The person building the analytics tracking may not be aware of changes that other departments make to the website, so those changes aren't covered in the initial tracking setup.

The ETL developer gets the information needed for the website launch, but no one communicates when a new landing page launches, impacting the clickstream data.

If you'll notice, all of these individuals are doing their jobs in their own internal worlds correctly, but they're failing on an operational level.

That's why you need to take an active role in designing processes that keep communication lines open.

Lack of Communication

Poor communication is almost always a culprit in data quality issues. I'm often amazed at how frequently stakeholders and team members alike are completely unaware of how they contribute to a successful data solution. These actions could be as simple as following prescribed naming conventions or using certain URL tracking parameters.

People often assume that other contributors automatically know what they're supposed to do based on some comment made several months prior. Or they assume that everyone reads documentation (hint: they don't).

It's important for everyone involved with data to adopt a mindset of overcommunication. That means if you know someone else will touch the data solution, over communicate to make sure they're ready for it and understand what their direct contribution is. If necessary, set aside time to train them on how to properly contribute to the solution.

Frequent Process Changes / Reorganization

Something you quickly learn about corporate America is how management loves reorganizing people. Quite often this is cited as a strategic decision to improve the company performance. You would think we were on the verge of world peace based on their level of enthusiasm for such changes. Really I think management just feels productive and effective when they change the org structure even if it doesn't result in meaningful impact to the bottom line.

Don't get me wrong. I think org changes and process changes are beneficial, but it's more the *frequency* that they occur that are an issue for me. If you have more than one org change a quarter (or even a year), then it's too much. If your process changes every month, then it's too frequent.

This is bad for data quality because it disrupts the natural flow of staff within an organization. More specifically, it disrupts the communication between supporting teams.

Let's say a website developer typically informs both the project management and the web analytics teams of an upcoming website launch date using JIRA. However, there's an org change, and he's told to send a ticket to the technical director via Trello moving forward. That way the technical director can approve the budget and then direct the web analytics team to start the work.

However, no one thought about the web analytics team and how to properly inform them. The technical director has to remember it's her responsibility now. But while the technical director is learning this new habit, costly mistakes are made. Web tracking promised to the client isn't delivered because the web analytics team wasn't informed.

Eventually the kinks in these reorgs resolve over time. But a lot of costly errors within the data happen because of them. So don't change things too often – no matter how productive it makes you feel as a manager.

Tight Deadlines

Tight deadlines warp the priorities of data teams. When they're told "we need this by the end of the day," important steps like requirements gathering and quality checking get rushed or skipped entirely. That means far more errors make their way through.

You can mitigate tight deadlines by breaking projects into smaller components and prioritizing the most important parts first. That allows you to still complete some critical processes we'll review later.

Employee Inexperience

Employees without much data experience usually cause a lot of headaches – for both themselves and their team. They tend to propose solutions that available tools can't support, implement hacks that aren't scalable, or rush projects to make a stakeholder happy. They also have an overly optimistic view about the accuracy of their data, reporting, and analysis.

Data, by its very nature, has little gremlins that employees handling it have to watch out for. This is why it's good to hire data workers with skeptical mindsets, because they are more vigilant for data gremlins. But even inexperienced employees with the same mindset tend to overlook how inaccurate their data can be.

They also overestimate their ability to use tools in a certain way. Typically, an inexperienced data worker is smart and creative. But they'll think up a creative solution and propose it

28

before verifying they can actually build it. They'll implement a hack to support the idea when the tool doesn't work as expected. Confession time: I'm guilty of this as well.

It's good to guard against inexperience by pairing new employees with more experienced ones. I also recommend not letting inexperienced employees lead requirement discussions until they've shadowed others for a while.

If you (the manager) are also inexperienced with data, it's good to quickly adopt a skeptical mindset of your own work. Assume your work is wrong and find ways to prove yourself right. Subject it to the same quality checking procedures that I outline in a later chapter.

Employee Error

Even the best, most experienced employees make mistakes. It's human nature and impossible to eliminate altogether. But you can get pretty dang close!

The best way a team can limit employee error is adopting a "the data is wrong until we can prove it right" mindset. Implement quality checking procedures and have employees check each other's work. Do this for every project. I'll cover this more in a later chapter.

Employee Incompetence

More often than not, data quality issues are blamed on employee incompetence. If this truly is the case, let that employee go or reassign them to a different role within the company. How do you know when it's time to do that?

If you've done everything else in this book to improve data operations, and you've set clear expectations, and you've noticed the same employee failing again and again, it's time.

Zack Pike, Callahn's VP of Data Strategy, said, "You should be talking to your team enough and watching what they're doing to know when they're succeeding and when they're not. If you have an analyst who's making quality mistakes so much that you have to measure it, it's my opinion that you need to find a new analyst."

My one caveat to Zack's advice is that I still recommend a project management tool to measure identified defects and attribute them to specific employees. If 80% of defects come from one employee, then you have a problem with one employee. But if defects come from all employees equally, you need better training or better processes. Or maybe you've just hit a defect equilibrium, where you literally can't reduce defects even further.

I caution against blaming employee incompetence too quickly or too often however. As I've said, most data quality issues are outside an individual's control and come from org changes, communication breakdown, inexperience, deadlines, etc.

I've heard many people throw their arms up in frustration with other departments saying, "Why don't they understand they're supposed to do this?" or "Didn't they read the documentation?"

Quite often "incompetent" people were never clearly informed of their expected contribution, never trained on how to properly contribute, and never received a straightforward, simple process to follow.

Be skeptical of yourself and your team when someone blames incompetence first. Verify that's really true before taking corrective measures, since it's much more likely you have an operational problem, than a people problem.

High Employee Turnover

Frequent turnover negatively affects data quality. Technological skills are mostly interchangeable, but data architecture and institutional knowledge are not.

A new employee must learn lots of new info like who knows what in an organization and where all the gremlins hide in a database. If there's frequent turnover, there are fewer experts to guide new employees through these imperfect systems.

This is so important to data quality that I wrote a whole chapter on how to reduce turnover and a separate chapter on salary, since it highly impacts an employee's decision to leave.

Disinterest of Management or Stakeholders

The highest quality reporting I ever produced was for a stakeholder with a bad attitude and the worst development process. He impulsively asked for requirement changes during quality checking and unfairly took his frustration out on my coworkers. If he ever bought and read my book, he would ignore the bulk of my advice.

But the data work we built for him was 100% accurate. To his credit, he understood that quality was everyone's responsibility. Even though this guy could be a jerk, he never saw errors as personal failure. He knew that was just the nature of data.

His team routinely followed up and thoroughly checked the work I delivered him. He also worked closely with his boss, who shared the same expectations of data perfection and understood the importance of quality to success in data.

When the people who use this data (such as stakeholders and upper management) think "good enough" is okay with data work, the people building those solutions just don't have the incentive to deliver quality work.

As a manager, demonstrate your commitment to quality work. Learn to build executive-level support from other departments and from your own CEO for data quality. Then individual contributors, both inside and outside your team, will take it seriously too.

What Won't Fix Data Quality Issues

Fixing data quality issues depends on your team adopting better processes and having management's support. However, many companies don't view these changes as viable.

Instead, they look for quick fixes, such as:

- Invest in a "better" or "easier" tool
- Hire "top performers"
- Conduct audits

These options can and do improve data quality, but there is a limit to their overall potential impact. Since most quality issues stem from operations, this foundation needs to be strengthened before such other methods can add incremental value.

Why Buying a "Better" Tool Won't Fix Your Quality Issues

There's an old saying that "only a poor craftsman blames his tools." This holds true in data work. There are some tools (cough, cough...Excel) that cause more errors than others, based on the volume of human inputs. But I've seen many perfectly good tools blamed for quality issues, when it's really an operational issue. Side note: go ahead and buy a new tool for improved functionality, but don't buy one because you think it'll improve data quality.

People will blame Tableau for quality issues and then buy PowerBI, even though both tools provide essentially the same functionality. Quite often there's a lack of understanding or skill about how to properly use the tool. Or the people using the tool are ill-suited to data work altogether. If a team member claims a new tool will solve their quality problems, I'd question their own data skills.

The best Tableau developers I know could and did learn other reporting tools. They will tell you there are tradeoffs to all platforms, but they're all essentially functional. The same holds true with ETL developers. If they learn SSIS, they can also learn Pentaho and use both effectively. The same with R and Python. When it comes to statistics and machine learning, both programming languages have trade-offs, but both perform the same functions effectively.

Inexperienced companies blame the tool and then become easy targets for sales teams for other BI tools. These salespeople use frustration to their advantage. Since it's so easy to blame the tool, companies may change frequently and buy each new tool that promises to do what they want and solve all their data problems.

Before buying a new tool, ask if your team is really using existing tools as thoroughly and correctly as they should. They might need more training, need better processes, or need to be replaced.

Hiring a Top Performer Won't Fix Data Quality Issues

If you manage to hire an entire team of top performers, you will likely see better results. But I think hiring such a team is statistically unlikely. Most employees, by definition, are within average performance of peers and competitors. So banking on finding top performers and letting them fix your problems is unrealistic.

You can probably hire one or two top performers (if you haven't already). One top performer will make a dent in quality issues, but only in their own work. There's a limit to how much their individual performance impacts others. Data quality issues are usually systemic, resulting from the broader business ecosystem. A top performer can't single handedly improve cross-department communication and the processes of other employees and stakeholders.

Instead, build a system that improves your average performer's quality through training and processes. Your top performer's time will naturally refocus to high-impact projects, rather than chasing down every last quality issue. Besides, you don't want top performers working on data quality. You want them working on finding cool insights!

Audits Only Improve Quality in the Short Term

Audits are usually necessary if you inherit a system from another team. I've conducted audits and observed many others conduct them as well. They often lead to a series of fixes and improvements. But if an audit doesn't fix the underlying issues with the business ecosystem, you'll find yourself repeating audits frequently. If you've found yourself auditing data more than once a year, you haven't fixed the real problem.

What Are the Best Ways to Improve Data Quality?

The best way to improve data quality over the long term is building organization-wide habits that all key players instinctively follow. Instead of something overly bureaucratic, they simply *do* key steps, such as requirements gathering, quality checking, and communicating with the necessary people. That happens when they know what's expected of them and are given the necessary support and incentives to complete those steps.

The best part is these habits also improve everything else on the *Data Success Pyramid.* So in addition to data quality improvement, you also see improvements in relevancy, readability, timely delivery, and stakeholder experiences.

My chapters *Habits (Processes) That Produce Success*, *How and Why to Gather Requirements*, and *How to Quality Check* will cover that extensively.

Outside of building these processes, there are a few other legitimate ways to improve data quality, including:

- Automate as much as possible
- Standardize tasks, output, and data
- Build a data dictionary

Automation Improves Data Quality

Humans have a natural tendency to make mistakes. Whenever they copy and paste data from one Excel workbook to the next, mistakes made now compound later.

Removing manual human inputs improves data quality. So instead of using Excel, build a data warehouse where data is automatically extracted, loaded, and transformed. Build reporting solutions with Tableau or other business intelligence software so no one has to manually produce reports on a regular basis.

When you automate, these solutions only have to be checked once or twice to verify their accuracy. Then they just *work* as programmed moving forward.

Find a way to automate or get rid of any manual data work, except for real analysis. If manual is your only option, build quality checks along the way to verify that manual inputs are accurate.

Be skeptical if a manual task can't be automated and someone says "we can't stop doing this." This happens often in reporting. For example, someone years ago demanded a PowerPoint deck with various metrics and analysis, delivered monthly.

Many, many times, the deck builders claim the apocalypse will start if they stop providing these PowerPoints. Then you ask the report recipients if they actually use it. They say, "Only slide three. We like the metric that reports how many website visits we get." And then you discover out of the long and arduous process of building those slides, on a weekly or monthly basis, only *one* metric even matters, and it could easily be sent in an automated report.

All the analyst had to do was ask.

The lesson? Ask stakeholders if a manual task is really necessary. If you explain that human input means the data is less reliable and not scalable, you'll be surprised how often they say you can get rid of it. Especially if you offer a better, automated alternative.

Standardization

Standardization is less critical when you have a small operation. But as your company scales up, you *must* standardize data architecture and tracking to support that growth. Also strive to standardize your company's output as well, such as websites, advertising, billing invoices, etc., so you can track it the same way consistently every time. Since this is a company-wide thing, you need to use influence and persuasion to gain support from other managers and executives.

Because steps are standardized, your employees can more easily implement them without making mistakes.

Also, standardization helps make the system more familiar. If a database developer must modify an existing database they've never used before, but it follows identical naming conventions as other company databases, it's easier for the developer to navigate and use it correctly.

Data Governance

A **data dictionary** is documentation defining each and every data point and how to properly use it. The document also defines how the data should look, so you can cleanse the data of bad data points.

I've thankfully never needed a data dictionary. I primarily work in digital marketing, which relies on various tools that define fields for us. I can't alter the definition of Facebook clicks, so I don't really bother defining it. Facebook already did that for me. I just make sure I know what it means and how it differs from Google Ad clicks.

That's not true though for most organizations. Nick Stevens, the chief data officer of the University of Kansas, shared a prime example.

"We have four different GPAs," he said. "You would think there's only one GPA, but no, there are four of them. So which GPA do you use when? Because we have all kinds of accreditation rules about whether we can use the plus or minus system. So is an A a 4.0 or does it have to be an A+?"

Whenever you have similar scenarios, data quality issues can develop because one developer uses one definition and other developers use a different one.

In these instances, a governing body that defines data fields and appropriate usage makes a major impact on data quality. You can also measure and report on how well the data meets those definitions.

"To me a data dictionary literally starts with the definition of a term," said Nick Stevens. "And then you track the data lineage of how that field is defined in that particular subject area or data model. Even with something as simple as an expense, we go through and define what that is. We describe where we pull that from and if we do any transformations to the data from the source systems."

The governing body would also include subject matter experts, according to Nick Stevens. "We engage them in order to get that context."

As the chief data officer, Nick directly oversees the governing body and is active in the process. That indicates how important executive-level support is to a data governance body.

If you decide your company needs a data dictionary and you want to delegate the responsibility to someone on your team, find a strong coalition builder who can lead such meetings and build executive-level support.

Things to Remember

- Data quality issues are a fact of life and your actions have an impact – whether you want them to or not
- Focus on process, automation, standardization, and data governance to improve data quality
- Data quality issues do not always result from employee incompetence, but instead are usually a natural byproduct of the business ecosystem

3

Habits (Processes) That Produce Success

Habits can be good or bad. Good habits make our lives better. Bad habits make them worse. People who eat healthy food and exercise regularly have far fewer health complications than people who don't.

Habits don't just apply to individuals. They apply to teams and organizations too!

Improving your team's habits improves the quality of your work and helps them *effortlessly* succeed on every level of the *Data Success Pyramid*. Issues with data quality, relevancy, and timely delivery almost always stem from breakdowns in communication and collaboration with stakeholders.

Good habits reduce these breakdowns.

What Do We Call Habits in the Business World?

We have a different word for habits in the business world: **processes**.

I never liked the term *process*. Process to me sounds bureaucratic. Something the office control freak invented to exert influence on others. After all, it's usually the office stick-in-the-mud who cites "process" the most when things don't go their way.

But a habit is not bureaucratic. It's natural. When someone does something habitually, they do it without forcing themselves to do it. And that's the end goal of a good process. To make it automatic and natural for your team.

Why Do We Want Processes to Become Habits?

Have you ever noticed when you don't brush your teeth before bed, your teeth suddenly feel slimy? What about when you don't wash your hands after using the restroom? Something just feels icky, right?

That's because our brain expects certain rewards from these behaviors. Our breath feels fresh after brushing our teeth. Our hands get a refreshing chill too. When we don't get those rewards at the expected time, something seems off.

You want your team's processes to feel like brushing teeth. It's a chore when they first learn it, but eventually the brain starts to expect it. At that point, it's no longer a chore. It's a habit, and they feel strange when they *don't* follow the process.

As a habit, the process isn't bureaucratic. It's not ignored or despised. It is simply followed habitually.

Why Do Habits Fail to Catch On?

A process fails to become a habit when the team doesn't follow it consistently for a long enough time. That usually stems from a lack of incentive, such as:

1. The process doesn't address an actual problem
2. The process doesn't seem important to the manager

The solution to the first point is simple: *don't make up pointless processes!*

The second one falls upon you, the manager, to fix. Data workers may get mixed signals from management. They're told, "Do good work, but do it quickly!" And they're told, "Get requirements, but don't upset the stakeholder by pushing too hard for a meeting!"

These mixed signals keep data workers from doing the little things that produce success.

As you recall from the pyramid of success, it's not good for data workers to prioritize stakeholder satisfaction and on-time delivery over quality, relevancy, and readability. But that's often the message from management, which ironically leads to stakeholder dissatisfaction in the long run.

Data workers know this isn't good, but they respond to what management indicates is important. If the boss asks "Why is this not done yet?" more often than "Why did you not gather requirements?" or "Why did you not quality check?", they will certainly prioritize speed over quality.

How to Avoid Creating Unnecessary Processes

Data workers love processes. You'll learn this fast, if not already. If they had it their way, they'd make up a process for everything! Including things that don't really need a process.

That might sound like a good thing at first, but it leads to process overload. The more processes you have, the less people follow them, including those that really do make a difference.

There are two reasons data workers create unnecessary processes.

The first is control. This isn't necessarily a power play though. Data workers naturally dislike chaos. It's why they're so good at their jobs. They want to organize things for maximum efficiency – from the code they write to projects they manage. Sometimes though a process they like works well for them personally, but less so for their colleagues, who find it stifling.

The second reason data workers love creating processes is far less noble – it deflects blame. Every once in a while, they'll make a random mistake, which embarrasses them. Rather than accept that they are human and can make mistakes, they'll say, "We need to update the process to account for this." That allows them to deflect blame from themselves to "the system."

Before you know it, these random errors lead to hundreds of new, detailed steps in the process, despite the fact that the errors don't actually happen that often.

Here's two general rules to prevent process overload:

- If an error happens more than once a month, create a process to prevent them
- If an error happens occasionally, don't create a process – just fix it and move on

What Needs a Process

Generally, a new process is needed when the following occurs:

1. Repeated output
2. Repeated errors

Repeated output means your team generates similar work on a consistent basis.

If your team provides data analysis every week for different stakeholders, then you need a process for handling how requests come in, how you interact with stakeholders, how you produce analysis, etc.

If your team builds new API connections on a regular basis, you need a process for researching APIs, gathering necessary credentials, etc.

Repeated errors also require a process.

For example, let's say your team depends on another team to upload data. You meet with the manager of that team, and they delegate it to new hires. After a few weeks, you notice the other team *consistently* uploads incomplete data. Even after you repeatedly point out the error to them. In that scenario, you could justifiably build a process to review their work to find missing data ahead of time.

How to Turn a Process Into a Habit

A process becomes a long-term habit when the team believes in it and they think their manager cares about it.

What's the simplest way to get the team to believe in the process? Include them in developing it!

Explain the problem you hope a new process will solve and seek their feedback. Ask them whether they noticed the problem too, what type of process would feel burdensome, what they think should be done, etc.

If your team feels involved in process development, they're more likely to buy into it. It'll feel less authoritarian and more democratic.

In addition to seeking their input, *prove that you care about it.*

Follow the process yourself and follow up on your team to make sure they're following it too. Since processes take time to become a habit, it's easy to forget key steps. Checking in on your team helps them remember to follow it.

You only need to do this for the first month or so after you start a new process, and you can lighten up after that.

Follow-up is needed because it signals you take this process very seriously and you will notice when it's not completed.

How to Delegate Process Development

Some managers are too busy to develop their own process, so they decide to delegate that process to a team member. That's fine, but you need to support that team member for success.

If you find yourself in this situation, encourage the employee to do what I outlined in the last section. First step, build enthusiasm from the team by soliciting feedback.

You still have a role to play during this. You must show support for their suggested process. When the employee presents their plan, you should open the meeting. You should indicate your support ahead of time. You then turn the meeting over to your employee to present, allowing them to get credit for the idea.

That approach gives the process the same chances of success as if you developed it directly.

What a Universal Process Looks Like for a Data Team

Every team is different, so processes tend to vary from one to the next. That being said, I find there's one universal process that lends itself to almost every data team out there.

This probably looks familiar, since it's commonly used in software development. It's also a strong starting point when you don't know where to begin with a process. Whether your team does analysis, data architecture, or report development, this process works. I still encourage you to tweak it to better suit your needs though.

Requirements

The end goal of requirements is building consensus among stakeholders and approving a requirements document.

Gathering requirements often include two stages: *discovery* and *requirements*. For simplicity's sake, I just call both *requirements*.

Done right, requirements is the longest stage of the development process. It usually involves several meetings with stakeholders. During that time, the analyst or developer on the project will also conduct additional research.

Does that sound like a lot of work? That's because it is. And requirements gathering is **where most data teams fail.**

As a manager, **you should absolutely make it clear that you prioritize requirements gathering** and that every project should have stakeholder approval on a requirements doc before moving forward.

If you and your team learn to succeed at requirements, you will see massive improvement on every level of the *Data Success Pyramid*. Since requirements gathering is the most important step of a project, I will devote **two whole chapters** on the topic.

Design

Many people confuse design with requirements, but they're different. Some people call design *technical requirements* and the previous stage *business requirements*. Two stages with the same word in them can lead to confusion, so I call it *design* instead.

Requirements are external facing and involve stakeholders. Design is mostly for internal planning. You will use this stage to draw a database schema, map out an ETL process, or draw a mockup for reporting. If it's an analysis project, an analyst determines what tests to run on the data.

This stage *usually* does not require interacting with stakeholders. One exception is for reporting projects. If that's the case, you will present a mockup to stakeholders for their approval.

Why is a dashboard mockup not a requirements document? Simple. You want requirements to focus on the *why*, *what's possible,* and *what's beneficial.* When stakeholders don't answer those questions first, they get carried away with design. Instead of talking about why a KPI fits their strategy, they start arguing over pie charts and bar charts. That's not very helpful to measuring a business strategy, is it?

Another common area where stakeholders need to participate in design is if their data engineer or developer will assist with data ETL. For example, you may need to connect to their systems to extract data. Based on experience working with the same data or systems, their developer can point out flaws in your approach ahead of time. And sometimes they won't even bother allowing you to connect without approval.

Development

Development is when your team actually builds something. It's when your employee puts on headphones and gets lost in the flow of building what is specified in requirements and design.

As you can imagine, this is the best part of a data worker's job.

If you spend enough time in the first two stages, development should only take a day or two. That's because your employee already mapped out everything. All the nasty surprises that plague most data teams (who don't gather requirements) were identified and considered ahead of time.

If a developer or analyst did not get good requirements, the projects will go into an endless cycle of development and revision, which can stretch a project out for months or even years.

I will *not* devote a chapter to development because this depends on your team's technical skills. Writing a chapter on this would require a detailed, technical manual on every possible tool you use, which your technology provider probably already wrote.

Quality Checking

Quality checking means another developer or a dedicated quality analyst reviews the project owner's work. This often gets skipped out of fear of missing deadlines and upsetting stakeholders. But as I've said before, quality is the foundation of long-term success in data.

As a manager, you should make it clear that quality checking is a **primary** responsibility for your team. No project goes to the client as "complete" without completing this step first.

Because of its importance, I devote an entire chapter to quality checking.

Production

Production is when work has been quality checked and deployed to an environment for the primary stakeholder to access it. For an analysis project, I call this stage *presentation*, where the analyst explains the results and provides recommendations, as well as any written documentation for the stakeholder to review as well.

A Note on Documentation and Why You Should Use a Project Management Tool

A lot of people feel the need to "document everything." Every time there's a slight oddity in a project, there's a race among team members to say "make sure you document that!" And every time an employee puts in a two-week notice, suddenly everyone and their mother demands the next great American novel's worth of documentation.

You *do not* need a separate task for documentation, and a departing employee really doesn't need to spend their last week documenting past work. The process I outlined above will take care of 95% of your documentation. But only if you consistently use a project management tool like JIRA or something similar.

Every time they get an approved requirements doc or design a schema, tell your team to upload it into the project management task for future reference. Make sure they use the project management tool for comments and record key points from real life conversations in the same task.

This reduces the need to do a separate documentation task. At worst, you should have your team write post-production release notes, which mentions any deviations from requirements or oddities found in the data.

Things to Remember

- The ultimate goal for processes is turning them into habits
- Processes become habits when the team sees the value and believe you (the manager) prioritize them
- A good process for data work typically includes:
  - Requirements
  - Design
  - Development
  - Quality Checking
  - Production
- Documentation throughout the project is easier in a project management tool using the above process

4

How and Why to Gather Requirements

I discovered quickly in my career that I had a special knack for gathering requirements. Many times on a project, other developers went in circles trying to anticipate and build what they thought stakeholders wanted. I took a different path – I met with those stakeholders and simply *asked* them what they wanted.

I cannot tell you how many weeks of development hours I saved from those one-hour meetings.

What's more, I could guide those stakeholder meetings with ease. Whether the stakeholder had a difficult personality or had no idea what they wanted from the data, I had no problem figuring out what they *needed* and delivering that to them.

I excelled here because I made it my purpose to **reduce ambiguity** surrounding project goals and what data was available to support those goals.

And that's the big theme of requirements gathering – **reducing ambiguity as early in the project as possible.** It's the most important skill in data work.

In fact, I say it's better to have a team with so-so technical skills that's great at requirements gathering, rather than a highly skilled technical team that's terrible at it. Obviously, you should try to have both whenever possible.

Requirements Gathering Is Where Most New Managers Fail

Managers without much experience in data underestimate the importance of requirements. I spoke with Tim Wilson, Senior Director at Search Discovery, who has consulted many years with companies on how to set up analytics practices.

"People have this vision that eighty percent of the [analyst's] time is spent on analysis and twenty percent of the time is on prep," he said. "I've watched managers who haven't come up through the analyst ranks be very befuddled when they learn how their team really needs to break up their time."

In order for projects to be successful, they'll need to spend 70% of a project's time in requirements and design. Since design is tool / work specific, I won't focus on how to accomplish that in this book.

"Just One More Adjustment" – What Happens When You Don't Gather Requirements

A project without requirements will almost *always* get stuck in development hell or abandoned altogether.

As you recall, a normal project development cycle looks a lot like this:

If you take out the requirements stage, the development cycle will look like this:

Let me give you a common scenario where this happens. A stakeholder emails the developer on Tuesday. There's a major push to build a report for her department and her boss wants it completed by the end of next week for a meeting with the CEO.

The developer asks what she wants on the report. She says her manager gave her some instructions, and she relays what she heard. The developer asks for some specifics, but the stakeholder says she doesn't know. She says she's also very busy this week, but she wants him to try his best and get started.

So the developer does just that.

The stakeholder sees what he's built a week later and says, "It's close. Could you do this too?" The developer makes an adjustment. Then the stakeholder reviews it and remembers another thing they need to include.

The developer adjusts it again. The deadline is now due, and they show it to the stakeholder's boss. Thankfully, the meeting with the CEO got pushed. But the boss says the report is not at all what she was expecting. She gripes and complains and asks for more adjustments.

The developer completes those adjustments. The boss takes it to the CEO and the developer thinks he's done. But then the original stakeholder starts to use the report. She complains about how it lacks this data or that data. Apparently she was so focused on making her boss happy that she didn't think about how she'd use it. So she asks for more adjustments.

Meanwhile, other stakeholders (and the boss) claim they keep finding errors in the data. The developer says it's accurate, but he had to decide on certain rules to clean up the data. That's why it doesn't match the source system exactly. These stakeholders ask for adjustments to his logic because they don't agree with the rules he made up without consulting them first.

This goes on and on until the report looks nothing like the developer's original work when he started – all because stakeholders keep asking for just "one more adjustment." Even worse, the stakeholders are now conditioned to think this is normal and expect the same process for future projects.

I once saw a two-month project turn into two years because the developer and stakeholder kept coming up with "another adjustment." All because they never bothered to get real requirements at the start of the project.

If you think I'm exaggerating, look at your current projects. Do any last longer than expected? Do people complain about going over budget and past deadlines? If so, take a look and see if you've had serious discussions and reached agreement on what to build. Did the project's developer or analyst effectively build consensus around requirements at the start of the project?

The answer is probably no.

Why Many Data Workers Avoid Requirements Gathering

Data workers love requirements, but most don't like gathering it themselves. This results from the mindset corporate America instills in people.

People tend to adopt a behavior that (they believe) reduces risk to their reputation. This looks similar to "keeping your head down." They believe if they say or do the wrong thing, their status will diminish in the eyes of their stakeholders and their team.

For that reason, these employees *avoid asking questions* that might make them look stupid.

So instead of confidently walking into a requirements meeting with questions, they sheepishly attempt to develop a solution before truly understanding the business problem. They spend tons of time guessing what the stakeholder wants and building a half-baked solution ahead of time. A solution which will need "one more adjustment" for eternity.

I've had several debates with coworkers about this tendency to avoid asking questions. Their response is "we're supposed to be the experts" or "we're supposed to come with solutions, not questions."

But there's a fundamental misunderstanding of what the word *expert* means in this context. You are a *business intelligence expert*, not a *subject matter expert*. Even if you specialize in the field of marketing (like me), you are still relatively clueless on how the decision makers are deploying their marketing strategy and what their goals are.

So when people say "we are supposed to be the experts with this kind of data," I respond that "I'm a marketing data expert. I should know what a session and a conversion is for a website. But I will never presume to know why a session or conversion is important to the subject matter expert."

Most Stakeholders Like Requirement Meetings

This fear of looking stupid in front of stakeholders is also misplaced. Most stakeholders LOVE requirement meetings. The biggest complaint from stakeholders is that the data they see is not actionable or relevant to them. Requirements gathering ensures that what you're delivering *is* actionable and relevant.

Remember that story I told about how stakeholders kept asking for "one more adjustment?" That's because they weren't happy with the results. A good developer would've asked them what their job entails and what information would help them. All of those stakeholders would've enjoyed sharing such info ahead of time.

Having a real conversation with stakeholders about what is important to them and their business questions makes them feel heard and part of the process. They'll also be more pleased with the final product because it answers their business questions and meets their expectations.

A stakeholder once told me that her goal was to build brand awareness. I asked her what a "successful brand awareness strategy" looked like to her. She lit up! She loved that question! And she became way more engaged in the conversation. Most people would be terrified to ask that because, "Shouldn't we know what successful brand awareness looks like?"

Stakeholders can also lose patience when you *don't* ask these questions. I once saw a lady lose her temper with a developer and scream in frustration, "What is it you need from me to do your job?!" I observed this developer during this whole process, and he had many opportunities to ask those questions. He didn't though. He just kept pitching solutions without asking questions.

Many data workers claim that stakeholders themselves are responsible for the lack of requirements. They say the stakeholders are too difficult and "don't want to have those types of conversations."

Yes. There are a handful of stakeholders that don't like requirements meetings. They are a small, *small* minority. Analysts and developers vastly overstate the frequency of this type of stakeholder.

You may reflect on my story about the developer and the group of "one more adjustment" stakeholders and say he tried to meet with them. And those stakeholders said they were too busy and wanted something by the end of the week.

What was he supposed to do, you might ask?

He could offer a compromise. He could say, "I can tell you're busy and you need something fast. What do you *know* you need this week? I can get that for you quickly in a spreadsheet." Then he could kick off a proper requirements gathering process the following week to develop a long-term solution.

And that's where most data workers fail with requirements gathering. They don't adapt their approach to bring stakeholders back into the conversation. They think requirements gathering is a clearly defined path with X amount of meetings and X amount of emails. That's not true. It's a soft skill and an art that many analytical people don't bother to learn.

They think because a stakeholder says "I'm busy this week" means "I'm busy forever." They must learn to push back *a little* in a *polite,* but *firm* way. They must learn to engage the stakeholder in a way that makes the stakeholder realize the importance of requirements.

When you learn to do this, stakeholders will be far happier with your approach and the results you deliver.

I devote a whole chapter to different types of stakeholders and how to handle the difficult ones who truly don't like requirements. Hint: you as a manager will have to back up your team when dealing with them.

How the "Not My Job" Mentality Impacts Requirements Gathering

Not every developer is afraid of requirements discussions. Some don't think it's their job at all. In their heads, they're a "doer" and not a "planner." They think someone else should provide those requirements, usually the stakeholder or project manager.

One developer (whom I actually respect deeply but disagree with on this point) told me, "When they tell you to dig a ditch, you dig the ditch. And when they tell you to fill the ditch, you fill the ditch. And then when they ask you why you filled the ditch, just remind them that's what they told you to do."

That mindset is costly in terms of development time – and a developer's time ain't exactly cheap!

The one scenario where it's okay for just one person to gather requirements and deliver to others is when you have *multiple* developers working on one project. You only need one real leader in requirements gathering. If you have multiple people doing it, it can become a confusing mess.

In these scenarios, the report developer or analyst should lead the requirement gathering process. They build the final product that other team members (such as web analysts and ETL developers) will support. So it's easy to start with the end product in mind and allow other team members to design their contribution based on that end goal.

Such scenarios are only common in large organizations, where your employees (or whole teams) specialize in one key area of the data journey. Too many developers in smaller companies still take on this mindset, however, when it's really not warranted or helpful.

And lastly, if someone keeps telling you to dig and refill the same ditch several times in a row, you need a different decision maker!

What Does Successful Requirements Gathering Look Like?

Good requirements gathering sets a solid direction for the project and reduces the number of delays during development. It typically occurs over several meetings, emails, and impromptu conversations. Requirements gathering ends with a requirements document, which the stakeholder approves before any design and development occurs.

In fewer words – a good requirements process ends with an **approved requirements doc**. The project does not move forward without it. No exceptions.

And the approved requirements doc is the only thing that's needed from a requirements phase. You can have as many or few meetings as you want, so long as there's an approved requirements document. That's where the *art* of requirements gathering comes into play and why many developers struggle with it.

What Makes a Good Requirements Doc?

A good requirements document is simple and easy to read. It isn't stuffed with bloated business jargon and avoids useless details, such as field type or a report's font and margin width.

The document typically focuses on the following:

- The solution's intended audience (CEO, executive, subject matter experts, etc.)
- Business questions or problems that the solution will solve
- Data sources
- For reporting projects:
  - KPIs that answer the business questions
  - Fields and dimensions that support those KPIs
  - Desired features, such as filtering and data visualization types
- For analysis projects, testable hypotheses that answer the business questions

You can see examples of requirements documents for both reporting and analysis on the next two pages. Both are available for download on my website, www.taylorrodgers.com.

Analysis Requirements Template

Analysis Requirements Document

A good analysis is one that focuses on hypotheses to validate. This document helps with that. While these steps may seem tedious at times, it ensures that whatever we produce has real value.

Discovery

Audience

Who will be using this analysis? Will it be a particular team? Or a vice president?

- (example: Accounting department)

Business Questions

What are the business questions you want to answer with this analysis?

- (example: Are we successfully increasing collection rates on past due payments?)

Requirements

Hypotheses

Down below, we take your business questions and rephrase them in the form of hypotheses. This allows us to better analyze the data and report our findings.

We believe...	If we are right, we will:	Data Source(s)
(example: Our new process for following up on past due payments is effective.)	(example: A significant reduction in past due payments.)	(example: Advantage database)

Considerations

Are there certain things we should know as we perform the analysis? Such as certain date ranges, specific actions you took that may skew results, etc.

- (example: January 30th is when we started the new process)
-

Results Delivery

How will we be presenting this information? PowerPoint? Over the phone?

- (example: we'll need someone to present to our entire accounting team during our weekly syncs)

58

Dashboard Requirements Template

Dashboard Requirements Document

A good dashboard is one that's focused on the business questions and delivers on expectations. This document helps with that. While these steps may seem tedious at times, it ensures that whatever we build you has real value.

Discovery

Audience
Who will be using this dashboard? Will it be your analyst? Will it be your vice president?
- (example: Financial Analysts)
-

Business Questions
What are the business questions you want to answer with this dashboard?
- (example: Are we successfully increasing collection rates on past due payments?)
-

Requirements

Big Picture Metrics
These metrics answer the 'big picture' of your business. This is where higher level executives will look first. If you have a single page dashboard, these are the metrics that are at the top or the far left. If you have a multi-page dashboard, these are the metrics that are on the first page.

Metric	Dimension	Data Source(s)

Lil' Picture Metrics
These metrics answer the little picture of your business. Analysts and subject matter experts will look at these sections since the data is at a more granular level. If you have a single page dashboard, these are the metrics that are at the bottom or on the right

59

hand side. If you have a multi-page dashboard, these are the metrics that are not on the first page.

Metric	Dimension	Data Source(s)

Filtering
Do you want the ability to drill down into certain categories or date ranges?
- (example: date range, default risk level)
-

Additional Features
Does seeing a map help you visualize what part of the country you need to take action in? Do you require a mobile version of your dashboard?
- (example: our executive is on the road a lot and would like a mobile version)

A stakeholder can easily read and understand requirements when presented this way. Once a developer gets the stakeholder's approval, they can then move to the design phase.

For this document, don't get too carried away trying to fill every single item out. The most important part for a reporting project is the list of fields, dimensions, and filters. If it's an analysis project, the hypotheses are the most important part. Other things are nice to know, but they won't derail the entire project if you don't get them.

How Do You Get This Document Filled Out?

There's no one-size-fits-all approach to getting an approved requirements document. It depends on the stakeholder's status within the organization, their personality, how much direction they have, etc.

Another chapter focuses on the stakeholder personas I've experienced. But when it comes to requirements gathering, these aren't hard-and-fast rules you must follow or else.

If it takes three meetings with stakeholders before you reach consensus, have three meetings. If it takes a single email, great. If the stakeholder walks up to you and gives you an exact list of fields, dimensions, and filters – perfect! They did your job for you!

So long as the stakeholder approves the requirements document and your developers verify they can build it, you can move forward on the project.

That said, I find data projects usually follow a path like this:

- Discovery Phase
- Internal Review
- Requirements Meeting (can be multiple)
- Follow-up Emails

Discovery Phase

The stakeholder reaches out to you or someone on your team. They send an email, log a ticket, or just walk up to your desk.

Sometimes the stakeholder walks up with a specific list of KPIs or has a simple analysis question. Or they might ask broader questions about the data you have without giving too many specific details about their goals.

If you sense there's a much bigger request hiding behind these questions, you can set up a discovery meeting. This is usually fifteen to thirty minutes. You ask for the "why" behind the request. On my requirement doc templates shared earlier, the information you learn during these conversations goes in the "discovery" section.

Here's a common conversation that occurs during the discovery phase:

> *Stakeholder walks up to the analyst's desk and taps him on the shoulder.*

Stakeholder: Do you have accounting data? Particularly the net income for product A? For the year 2019?

Analyst: I think we do, but I'd have to check. Let me write that down. But before we get too involved, what is it you're trying to do?

Stakeholder: I just want to know how well product A has sold. Nothing else. I'm just seeing what's possible.

Analyst: That's all? I can query that data and send it to you before lunch today. But what made you want to ask this?

Stakeholder: Well… we were thinking of discontinuing product A. We haven't decided yet. I think it's just that we haven't allocated the right marketing budget for it since product B is similar and is selling fine. I just need to know if product A is really that bad of a performer. Now that I think about it... I guess I need product B's performance too so that we can compare the numbers.

Analyst: Ah! That's interesting. I'll send you preliminary numbers for both product's performance today. But we can do a much more thorough job here and really see if product B performs that much better and if so, whether it's the marketing spend or not. Would you be willing to sit down for a longer meeting later today? I'll do more research on the data we have and we can discuss what all you and your team thinks is impacting this product's performance.

Stakeholder: Really? That would be great! My boss won't be able to make it and I think Keri is out of the office this afternoon. I'll ask real quick on what they think the problem is and I'll bring my notes.

You'll likely notice the stakeholder throws out some hypotheses to test. But more importantly, the analyst is able to understand the *why* behind the request and determines ahead of time that it's an analysis project. The business problem is, "Product A doesn't seem to sell well, and we want to know if we should discontinue it or not."

Developer Review Time

Developer (or analyst) review time happens in tandem with both the discovery and the requirements meeting(s). As the developer or analyst learns more information about what the stakeholder wants, they research what's possible and what isn't. They also begin to fill out the requirements document with suggestions on what KPIs or hypothesis questions should solve the business problem.

In the prior example, the analyst learns they need to know at least net income for product A and product B, as well as the marketing budgets for both. He needs to research if that data is available.

He could stop there and probably satisfy the stakeholder, but I would research what other data is available that could help answer the business problem. He may discover there are various components to the marketing budget, such as TV, digital display, radio, etc. He might use that as the basis of his analysis and suggest a hypothesis such as, "If we spent the same on TV for product A as we did product B, then we'd expect to see equal performance." He could expand that further and suggest, "If we spent X on TV, X on digital display, and X on radio, then we'd expect to see equal performance."

These are all things that should be documented on the analysis requirements doc.

Requirements Meeting

The requirements meeting is what most people think of when they think "requirements gathering." Usually this is when the developer can form a consensus among stakeholders (sometimes with competing agendas and viewpoints) and agree on the project's desired outcome.

To maximize effectiveness in these meetings, a developer should do the following:
1. Send an agenda
2. Send unresolved questions for stakeholders to review
3. Send a version of the completed requirements document ahead of time

Typically, developers find barriers or issues with the data they research during developer review time. They may also get competing and conflicting directions from various stakeholders during discovery conversations. Send these questions in the agenda, so stakeholders can review ahead of time and know they must be settled by the end of the meeting.

Suggest-and-Vote Usually Leads to Requirements Approval

During a requirements meeting, the **suggest-and-vote** method is the easiest way to get an approved requirements document, especially if there are multiple stakeholders.

Typically, the stakeholder only provides a business problem or business question. They don't know what KPIs to report or hypotheses to test.

The developer should use what they discover during internal review time to create a list of applicable KPIs or hypotheses. They should then create a rough draft of the requirements document with that information filled out.

If a developer writes out their suggested ideas, as well as any others that stakeholders suggested, the stakeholder group can then vote to accept or reject each one of the suggestions.

This is a much better way to build consensus than asking "what KPIs do y'all want?!"

Follow-Up Meetings or Emails

I find the suggest-and-vote method *usually* ends with a consensus and an approved requirements document at the end of the first meeting. But not always. Sometimes a new detail comes up and the developer needs to do more research. Or the stakeholders think of one other person to loop in before approval.

That might require an additional meeting or a follow-up email, but that's not the norm. Usually one requirements meeting is enough.

Once the stakeholder approves the requirements document, you can move forward to the design phase – where you design mockups, decide experiment formats, and design database schemas.

Note: if you design a dashboard mockup, you need another meeting with stakeholders for them to approve the design.

You Won't Always Need a Requirements Meeting

You could realistically not need a requirements meeting at all. Sometimes you'll get that rare stakeholder who is proactive with their own research. They'll come to you with a requirements document (or something similar) filled out ahead of time. They'll also give you their ideal completion date and ask if you can complete it by then. When that happens – celebrate! The data gods have smiled favorably upon thee and you can move forward with the project.

As you can imagine, that doesn't happen often. One CEO told me if that happened every time, most of us wouldn't have jobs. And he's probably right.

Requirements Also Allow You To Avoid the Reporting Trap

Requirement discussions are a good time to avoid the reporting trap. The **reporting trap** is where stakeholders and developers focus on reporting KPIs and inadvertently miss providing real analysis. One analyst told me he calls this "reporting hell."

I used to blame the stakeholder for this more than the data workers. I thought the stakeholder should say if they have a one-off question, as opposed to needing a full-blown dashboard. After all, we're reliant on stakeholders to tell us what they need, right?

But I've changed my thinking on this over time.

Stakeholders typically don't know what a good analysis question looks like and why it differs from a KPI. They don't know what is possible with data analysis in general. They don't know what a t-test is or a regression analysis is either.

But these stakeholders often read in trade articles that data is important and they *need* it. So they ask for a dashboard and KPIs, because that's all they know when they think of data. What these stakeholders really need is guidance.

Data workers *can* and *should* provide that guidance – and there's no better time to do that than requirements.

How Tim Wilson Gathers Requirements to Streamline Reporting and Focus on Analysis

I give Tim Wilson, Executive Director at Search Discovery, credit for showing me how to escape the reporting trap. I interviewed him (like many other people) while researching this book. He uses requirement discussions to generate analysis projects and streamline reporting projects. He calls them hypothesis validation and performance measurement, respectively.

"A performance measurement tends to be recurring," he said. "There needs to be a daily or weekly or monthly reporting. There aren't really insights tied to it. It's literally just we're on track or we're not in these specific areas."

"Hypothesis validation is inherently not on a schedule," he went on to say. "You don't get weekly insights about your website because you're not changing your website every week."

He told me he'll build a *hypothesis library* with one-off questions mentioned during requirement gathering. You can use a hypothesis library if you want (which is basically a Google Sheet) or you can use my analysis requirements template. Both work fine.

Basically, requirements for reporting can generate requirements for analysis projects – even if the stakeholder doesn't come to you with that purpose.

After you build and automate reporting, you can then focus your work on testing hypotheses that surface during those conversations.

Many stakeholders complain that reporting alone doesn't generate much value – and they're right! Identifying analysis projects with this approach generates far more value for your stakeholders, helping you truly become "data-driven."

And you'll be more impactful than most other data teams out there!

How to Tell What's an Analysis Project and What's a Reporting Project

It's actually easier than you think. My general rule is that an analysis project is a one-off question that a stakeholder won't ask frequently. It doesn't require automation. A reporting project involves KPIs that people need to monitor frequently.

An analysis project can be rephrased as a hypothesis. Tim Wilson uses the "If we change A, then B will happen" format.

For example, let's say a stakeholder states they recently changed the picture on a display ad. Their art director swears the new picture leads to more clicks on the ad. The account executive doesn't like the picture though and thinks most people just scroll past the ad.

That debate becomes a testable hypothesis: "If we change the image on the display ad, then we expect more ad clicks."

It's that easy.

And you can discover and build a hypothesis list if you just learn how to guide stakeholders in that direction during requirement discussions.

What Happens If My Stakeholder Keeps Changing Their Mind?

The indecisive stakeholder is a challenge for both new and experienced developers. These stakeholders usually lack vision or fear they'll forget a key component. Also, they usually don't realize the significant cost in development hours from their indecisiveness.

This problem is more common with report and database development than analysis projects, since analysis projects are more flexible.

I find effective requirements gathering and over communication takes care of the bulk of indecisive stakeholders. But for stakeholders who continue changing their minds, I take a different approach.

I tell them what we're agreeing on is "version 1." It won't be the end-all-be-all for their reporting needs. I tell them if they forget about something, it's perfectly acceptable to revise the dashboard for version 2.

I even let them know we can start on version 2 as soon as we finish quality checking version 1. But we should agree on version 1 and complete it first, so they get something that works and provides value more quickly.

Once they realize the requirements document isn't the final word and the dashboard can be improved in the future, few stakeholders are still as indecisive afterwards.

I used this tactic for a stakeholder with a reputation for indecisiveness. I inherited a dashboard cluttered with KPIs and an abundance of quality issues. It took a long time to load and open too. My boss told me the executive stakeholder kept asking for additions and changes. This lasted months until finally the CTO said enough. My boss made her sound super difficult to work with.

A few months later, I was building a new dashboard for her and her team. I explained version control and the development process upfront. I said what we build doesn't have to be the end product. As you use it and think of improvements, we can build a version 2.

The result?

We built this dashboard in one month's time and had absolutely no complaints or re-works. She felt more comfortable we wouldn't "miss" something the first time because we could be flexible in future versions. And she was nowhere near as difficult as my boss had made her sound.

Things to Remember

- Good requirements gathering reduces ambiguity about a project's outcome and goals
- Good requirements gathering ends with a stakeholder-approved requirements doc
- Good requirements gathering sets every project up for success
- Most stakeholders love requirements gathering
- Most data workers need coaching on how to gather requirements
- You can use requirements gathering to "escape the reporting trap" by classifying and approaching requests as reporting projects or analysis projects (or both)

5

How to Work With (Almost) Any Stakeholder to Gather Requirements

I always thought the term *collaboration* was a bit corny. Businesspeople use it frequently. It gets tossed around as the solution to every problem.

It's especially odd when applied to BI development and analysis work. That type of work requires one individual focusing, studying, and developing a solution using data. Forced collaboration prolongs the development for those projects – especially if it's within the same tool for the same project.

But one area where collaboration is legitimately needed is requirements gathering. You must learn to work with stakeholders of various types of skill, intellect, influence, and personality to generate real value for the organization.

And as cliche as I feel saying it, collaborating with stakeholders is a lot of fun. It is legitimately my favorite part of this job. Whether the stakeholder has a challenging personality or not, I love the process of building a consensus with them. It's the only time I really feel like my work generates real value, and I have never (well, almost never) met a stakeholder I didn't like.

Many Data Workers Don't Accommodate Stakeholder Personalities and Work Preferences

In the last chapter, I said developers love requirements but don't like to gather them directly. Many assume the stakeholder should simply provide straightforward requirements and complain when they don't. I've seen many developers, generally friendly people, say viciously nasty things about stakeholders because the stakeholders didn't know or ask for exactly what they want during the first meeting.

This stems from the logical thought process many data workers take with their work. They think A naturally leads to B and nothing else will. If the stakeholder doesn't follow the prescribed process to the most minute detail, then the stakeholder is the problem.

But that's just not how the real world works. Each stakeholder is unique and requires a different approach to tease out what's needed to solve their specific problem.

So when it comes to requirements gathering (where the bulk of stakeholder interaction occurs), tell your team this: *the end goal of requirements gathering is a stakeholder-approved requirements document. But adapt your approach as needed based on the stakeholder.*

Yes. Sometimes It Really Is the Stakeholder's Fault

Maybe it was my four years as a retail assistant manager, but I've always been big on customer service and the whole "the customer is always right" mindset. I tried to apply that to data work and now call it "stakeholder service." This enables me to succeed with projects and generate real value when many other data workers don't.

But there is a limit. Some stakeholders are responsible for the project's failure. And that's not the fault of the developer.

That's why I use the word "stakeholder," even if the work I deliver is for a paying client. Stakeholder indicates a collaborative partnership and a collaboration is only as good as the collaborators involved. If the stakeholder collaborates poorly and doesn't have the necessary knowledge or skills to do so, your developer won't produce good work. Period.

The Two Stakeholder Spectrums

There are a million ways to categorize stakeholders. Salespeople like to create fictional personas (like "Dan the Doctor") that indicate how to best tailor the sales pitch for different audiences. We can take a similar approach in data work.

I have two spectrums to effectively categorize stakeholders:
1. Low Direction to High Direction
2. Low EQ to High EQ

Low Direction to High Direction Spectrum

The **low direction to high direction** spectrum denotes the stakeholder's vision for a project. Do they know how they'll use the data? Do they have specific business questions to answer? Did they ask for this project directly or did someone delegate it to them?

Low Direction ← ——————————————————— → High Direction

A stakeholder with low direction never proposes their own KPIs or hypotheses to test. They usually don't know a specific business problem to solve with the data either. In other words, they want data...they just don't know what for.

A stakeholder with medium direction probably knows the business question or problem to solve. They just don't know what's actually possible with the data. They hope you can provide that guidance.

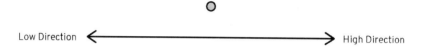

A stakeholder with high direction knows exactly what KPIs or hypotheses to test and dictates them to you. This isn't a bad thing, per se. It means your team can deliver the work immediately, after verifying data exists to support the request. If the stakeholder is willing to discuss, you can ask the *why* behind the request as well. You may find ways to add even more value on top of their request.

Low EQ to High EQ

The **low EQ to high EQ** spectrum references the stakeholder's emotional intelligence. Are they nice? Or a total jerk? Are they blunt and frequently interrupt others? Or do they communicate clearly and politely?

A low EQ stakeholder is almost always incredibly rude. Usually their communication style makes it very difficult to work with them. They may yell at your team or complain negatively about them when they're not around. Sometimes they aren't mean, but instead their social awkwardness makes it impossible to communicate with them.

A medium emotional intelligent stakeholder is just a bit odd. Or their behavior goes against the office culture. They may communicate clearly, but may not be very considerate or conscientious. They respond to an email, but it's a direct, short sentence that comes off rude. Or they often interrupt people unintentionally.

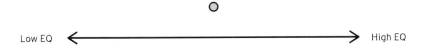

A high emotional intelligent stakeholder is who everyone either loves or at least respects. They send emails that are easy to read and understand. They have agendas for meetings and kick off every project with, "What can I do to make your job easier?"

Combining the Two Spectrums

When you turn the low-direction-to-high-direction spectrum into a Y axis and overlap with the low-EQ-to-high-EQ spectrum, you get the plot below:

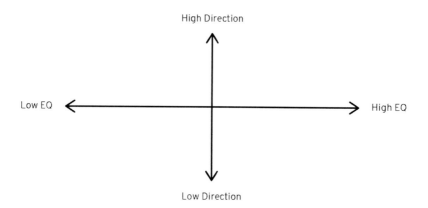

Now you can effectively plot your stakeholders and adapt your approach accordingly.

Stakeholder Type: Low Direction / High Emotional Intelligence

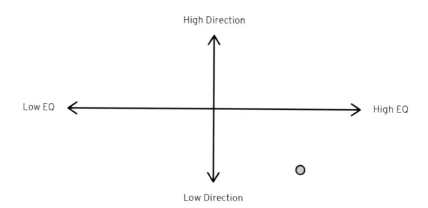

A stakeholder who doesn't know what they want from a data solution is challenging. They change their minds (a lot) and always ask for just "one more adjustment."

But you're in luck if a low direction stakeholder has high emotional intelligence. You can brainstorm ideas together. They'll also become better at giving directions over time. But you will spend more time in requirements gathering than other stakeholders.

Usually these stakeholders are simply novices to data strategy. They know data is important, but they just don't know how to use it yet. Maybe they were delegated the responsibility of managing the project. Their boss asked them to work with the data team (you) to produce more valuable data for their business needs. Only the stakeholder isn't exactly sure what data or insights they even need.

Sometimes this problem impacts the whole organization. The board of directors or investors realize competitors are investing in data. So they tell the CEO to become "data driven." The CEO doesn't know what that actually means, but hires a handful of data scientists and tells them to deliver insights.

Because leadership doesn't provide clear direction on business challenges, developers guess what type of work delivers value. Some naively wing the project and deliver a solution, but then get lost in the "one more adjustment" spiral. Or they simply don't do anything at all and bluntly tell the stakeholder "think about what you want and get back to me."

Neither approach generates a good stakeholder experience.

Don't expect low direction stakeholders to propose their own KPIs or hypotheses to validate. Focus on a different area that they can conceptualize.

When working with these stakeholders, focus on *discovery* more than *requirements*. As I said in the last chapter, discovery focuses on business strategy. Real requirements generate from that discussion.

What does that mean in a practical sense? Coach the stakeholder to ignore the data solution altogether. Don't worry about becoming data-driven. Don't try to force thinking up KPIs or hypotheses.

Instead, encourage the stakeholder to answer these questions:

1. What business questions do you often ask yourselves?
2. What types of business problems do you face?
3. How do you define success for your team or organization?
4. How do you define success for your current projects or business strategies?
5. How does your team define success in their day-to-day output?
6. What are the biggest pain points for your business?
7. What is a major internal debate in your team or organization? What do you think is the correct answer in that debate?

As stakeholders answer these questions, your analyst starts searching for data to understand and solve the team's business problems. The analyst then proposes KPIs or hypotheses and allows the stakeholder or group to vote on them.

For example, a CFO asks an accountant to work with the data team to generate reporting for the accounting department. The accountant doesn't know why that's necessary though. They seem to operate just fine without working with the "data geeks."

The accountant schedules a meeting with the data team and asks, "What is it you can do?"

The developer could respond by asking about various daily tasks. Does the accountant compile reports? If so, how much time does that take? You could potentially automate these reports and free up time for more important tasks.

The developer could also ask about common frustrations for the accounting team. Not with data, but just with the day-to-day job. Do clients pay their bills on time? Do project managers indicate when projects are complete and need to be billed? Business intelligence offers solutions to both those problems.

For this stakeholder type, ask about business problems and ignore KPIs and hypotheses altogether. In shorter words, you're moving this stakeholder along the curve to becoming a medium-direction stakeholder.

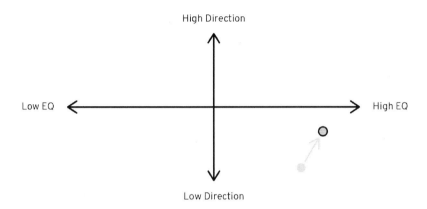

With low direction high EQ stakeholders, only assign experienced data team members. Preferably those who've worked at your company awhile. They know the data systems better and can help brainstorm legitimate ideas with the stakeholder faster. You set newer developers up for failure if you ask them to lead these discussions. Feel free to let them attend the meetings though to learn how to work with this stakeholder type.

Stakeholder Type: Medium Direction / High Emotional Intelligence

This stakeholder is the most fun to work with, in my opinion. They are good collaborators and allow you to exercise more creative control over your work.

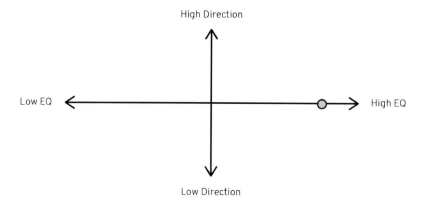

Typically, a medium direction and high emotional intelligence stakeholder knows what they know and what they don't know. Instead of trying to guess their own KPIs or hypotheses, they'll bring you a predefined business problem or question. They'll then ask you to help solve the problem with data.

More experienced team members should still handle these stakeholders, but it's okay to assign someone less experienced in some instances. This stakeholder shows a great deal of patience and should be less irritated if you assign a newbie who needs more time for research.

Typically, this stakeholder happily follows the standard process I outlined in my last chapter:

1. Discovery Phase
2. Internal Review
3. Requirements Meeting
4. Follow-up Emails

With these stakeholders, it's best to use the "suggest and vote" method for KPIs and hypotheses. Since they don't know the data and how it possibly answers their business problems, they require suggestions. They're usually astute enough with their own business needs to accept or reject your suggestions. After that, you can move straight into development.

Stakeholder Type: High Direction / High Emotional Intelligence

These are the best stakeholders in the world. They typically fill out a requirements form themselves (or send the information you need to fill it out) without additional meetings.

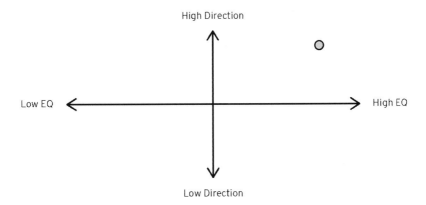

Many data workers naively assume all stakeholders should be like this, but there'd be far fewer data jobs if that were the case.

When you get these stakeholders, you can often begin work immediately on the project and complete it quickly. That makes the stakeholder especially happy if it's a short deadline.

However, if there's not a hard deadline, I suggest asking the stakeholder about the business problems and questions behind the request. If they send you an exact list of KPIs, they may not also provide related background info.

Asking for this background info helps you think of even better data to answer the underlying question. Data the stakeholder didn't even know existed. While they know they can get KPIs, they may not know you can build a predictive model to answer their business questions with more certainty.

These stakeholders love when you're able to offer more than they asked for.

Stakeholder Type: High Direction / Low Emotional Intelligence

We all know that talented person who's also insanely difficult. You sometimes wonder if that goes hand-in-hand. This type of stakeholder knows exactly what they want, but their communication skills make it challenging to interact with them. Any slight error will send them raging at you.

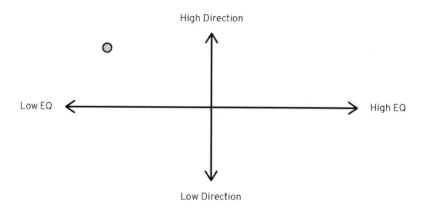

The most famous example of one of a high direction, low EQ stakeholder was Steve Jobs. The man had remarkable vision and built one of the most successful companies ever. He was also a real jerk. He somehow managed to get fired from his own company because he frustrated the board of directors so much.

Quite often, developers don't like this stakeholder and claim they're impossible to work with. That's not true. You just need a thick skin and you must stay calm no matter what they do.

Unlike their high direction, high EQ counterpart, you can't really ask them the business questions and problems behind the request. They get grumpy when you do. They also don't like suggestions or feedback. They view it as criticism.

That leads to a problem where you build a solution to their specifications and then they claim you forgot something, when really they forgot to tell you about it in the first place.

For that reason, it's important to leave a paper trail – especially a requirements document. They often refuse to fill this out and may not even look at it, but as you gain direction from them via communication, fill one out anyways. Then send an email saying "this is what we'll be building. If anything is missing, let us know by tomorrow. Then we'll get to work."

That way there's proof of some agreement and you gave them a chance to confirm or deny the requirements.

Stakeholder Type: Medium Direction / Low Emotional Intelligence

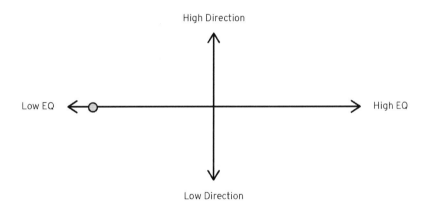

It's difficult to have a productive relationship with a medium direction, low EQ stakeholder. They have a business problem or business question, but when you attempt to probe and follow the "suggest and vote" method, they get angry and frustrated. They think you should just go figure it out.

With these stakeholders, you as a manager *must* back up your team. Whenever these stakeholders complain to you (or others in the company), simply state they must follow the established process like everyone else.

Just like their high-EQ counterpart, the best process with these folks usually follows these steps:

1. Discovery Phase
2. Internal Review
3. Requirements Meeting
4. Follow-up Emails

Just expect these stakeholders to be grumpy the entire way through. They'll let you know it too.

Stakeholder Type: Low Direction / Low Emotional Intelligence

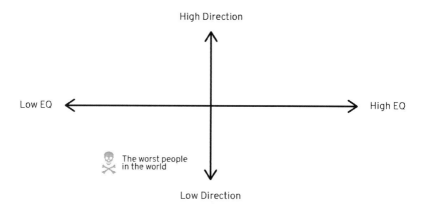

There's only one stakeholder you can't work with at all and that's the low direction, low EQ stakeholder. These are the folks who have absolutely no vision for their project, can't provide any guidance on what they want to accomplish, and are the biggest jerks you'll ever meet.

I've only ever met one stakeholder in this category, which tells you just how rare they are. I worked with this stakeholder directly after two other developers either quit or got fired. I couldn't deliver results either. The guy never showed up to meetings. Another developer tried after me and didn't have any luck either.

My boss told me the stakeholder was right to be angry with the poor results. I responded "four separate people have tried and failed. You can't blame all of that on employee incompetence."

The most frustrating part is not realizing you're dealing with this stakeholder type until you've already wasted several meetings with them. They often schedule meetings, cancel them, show up and complain, complain to other people, yell at you, and won't offer any guidance or answer any questions. Even though their behavior is the only common denominator, they somehow deflect blame entirely on everyone else involved.

As a manager, you must absolutely back up your team when dealing with these rare stakeholders.

Things to Remember

- Adjust your approach to requirements gathering based on the stakeholder's sense of direction and their emotional intelligence
- For stakeholders with a low-to-medium direction, focus on getting them to state business problems and questions so you can then pitch solutions
- For high direction stakeholders who provide an exact list of KPIs or hypotheses, ask for additional context so you can provide more value
- For low-EQ stakeholders with medium-to-high direction, remain calm and nudge them into the process. Use documentation to hold them accountable, as they're more likely to blame you for their mistakes
- For low direction, low EQ stakeholders, recognize that the project won't succeed, and it's best to mitigate their ability to hurt your team's reputation for good work

6

How to Quality Check

In simplest terms, quality checking ensures you deliver what you promise to your stakeholder and the numbers are as accurate as humanly possible.

Doing this consistently improves the stakeholder's experience and trust in your abilities. Failing to do this means stakeholders stop trusting your data and you personally.

Many data workers struggle with quality checking for a handful of reasons. It may be the manager's fault. They may institute unreasonable deadlines or consistently fail to support their team when needed.

Other times, it's the employee's fault. They may fail to gather proper requirements or fail to include others in the quality checking process.

And sometimes, it's the *stakeholder's* fault. They may consistently ignore your process and ask for multiple changes midway through quality checking, thus blurring the line between feedback and requirement changes.

All of these reasons are within your power as the manager to fix.

Why Should You Quality Check?

The human brain isn't perfect. When you are so wrapped up in building something, it's challenging to notice errors that are glaring to outsiders.

Think back to your college years. You probably wrote several papers for various courses. If you waited until the day before a paper was due, the paper probably wasn't that good.

However, when you wrote a rough draft a week early and reviewed it the day before, you probably spotted many errors. You then probably had an easier time improving it to get a higher grade.

The reason is your brain could reset. This same principle makes quality checking so important. With deadlines, we don't have time to allow our brains to reset and view our work like it was new again.

For that reason, we need to help one another quality check work.

Quality Checking Involves Two People

You can follow a simple checklist to quality check your own work, but thoroughness is unlikely, especially on a short deadline. For that reason, quality checking works best with two people involved – the developer and the quality checker.

This doesn't mean you need to hire someone to quality check full time though. It means your team should swap roles from project to project. When Developer A builds a solution, Developer B should quality check it. When Developer B builds a solution, then Developer A should quality check it.

Make Quality Checking a Primary Responsibility

The problem with quality checking is not that people don't see the value in it. Every data worker has a story of an embarrassing error showing up after deployment. The problem is they're often incentivized to not burden co-workers with quality checking tasks and push work to production as soon as possible.

As a manager, you must build a culture of quality on your team and elevate quality checking as a primary responsibility of all developers, not just a "nice-to-do" when time allows.

It's Normal to Feel Some Anger During Quality Checking

Ask any quality analyst and they'll tell you about nasty reactions they've received to their feedback. It's human nature. Any time you work hard on something, believe it's perfect, and then receive a list of corrections, it's easy to get a little angry (initially).

I'm not even immune to this reaction. I regularly preach the gospel of quality checking, institute it as a process, and then think "what the hell is this jerk's problem" when a co-worker points out my mistakes during that same process.

But then I take a deep breath and realize – I made mistakes and my co-workers are helping me do right by the stakeholder.

More experienced employees recognize this as well, but you may have to coach newer employees ahead of time to prepare them. Tell them it is normal to feel frustrated during quality checking and the other person is helping them do a better job. And lastly, their competency is not in question based on a mistake caught during quality checking.

Don't Let Conflicting Employees Quality Check Each Other's Work

Employees who don't like each other should not quality check each other's work. They may use the opportunity as a power play to "get back" at the other employee for some perceived slight.

Sometimes this is just one employee's perception, but it can create discord nevertheless.

Quality Checking Is Not a Place to Change Requirements

I've upset many co-workers during quality checking by not implementing requested changes that don't relate to quality. Many people mistakenly believe that quality checking is a time for general feedback, such as changing chart types, using different KPIs, or applying a different color scheme.

I've often just flatly said no to these requests. Why? Quality checking is to ensure what you built meets the original requirements – not accommodate the quality checker's personal preferences. If the stakeholder requests a particular KPI, it's not the quality checker's prerogative to change it.

However, there's nothing wrong with quality checkers making suggestions on improving the work. It's possible the quality checker (as the first user) recognizes a concept doesn't really work out as expected. In that instance, they can recommend a change, which the developer must clear with the stakeholder. Quite often the stakeholder will agree with the quality checker.

Which brings me to my next point...

The Developer Doesn't Have to Implement Every Change

Some quality checkers believe their word is final and all feedback must be implemented. That's not true. If the quality checker finds errors, the developer must fix them. But if the quality checker offers helpful suggestions or improvement ideas, the developer can use their own judgement.

When I quality check other people's work, I classify feedback into two categories: **must fix** and **suggested changes**. That's a little less insulting to the developer as well.

Here's an example:

Must Fix
- *Sessions KPI doesn't match the bar graph below.*
- *The date parameters don't apply to all visualizations.*
- *The company color scheme isn't on all bar graphs.*
- *Custom calculations don't have very clear naming conventions.*

Suggested Changes
- *Custom calculations for predicting revenue are a bit confusing. I would add some comments for future developers, explaining how they work. Or link to a google doc that explains it.*
- *KPIs are a bit large for their boxes. Just my opinion, but it might help to make them a bit smaller.*
- *The bar graph label "Revenue for Year [p.Year] and Month [p.Month]" is a bit awkward. Maybe try "Revenue for [p.Month]/[p.Year]"?*

Use a Project Management Tool

Make sure all quality checking feedback and comments are captured in a project management tool. It's a handy reference and resource for future developers to troubleshoot a project. I've had to extensively troubleshoot SQL stored procedures and reports and that additional info provides a lot of critical context missing from requirement documentation.

Use a Quality Checklist If You're New to Quality Checking

I don't use a quality checklist anymore when I review other people's work. Eventually, you just naturally know how to quality check. But newer employees need more guidance. When I train someone new for quality checking, I provide a validation checklist.

My list is extensive but not all items apply to every situation. Eventually, the employee can quality check without referencing the list. I provide generic checklists by role at the end of this chapter for your use.

While each type of data work involves different quality checklists, some common checks exist across all of them. Those include:
1. Data matches the source system
2. Data duplication does not occur
3. A leads to B consistently
4. Math is correct

Data Matches the Source System

You should always check your data solutions against the earliest source data possible, preferably before any data manipulation occurs.

Let's use a reporting solution as an example.

Picture how your data flows from one object to the next. Does it go through several databases and stored procedures before it appears in reporting?

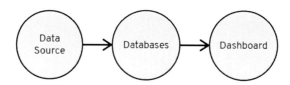

For example, I work in marketing and often deal with website data from Google Analytics.

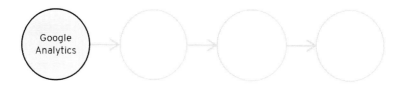

Then the ETL developer pulls and stores that data in a database.

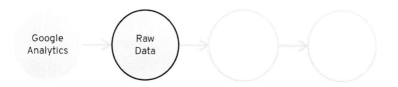

Let's say I decided to compile my GA data with other data. I build my own reporting tables within a SQL database to make it easier for my reporting tools to read.

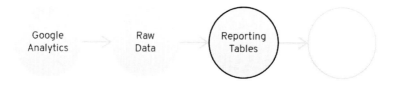

Then my dashboard pulls data from those reporting tables. And we now have the data journey completely mapped out.

Ideally, I check my final dashboard against Google Analytics since my stakeholder will likely check against that source as well.

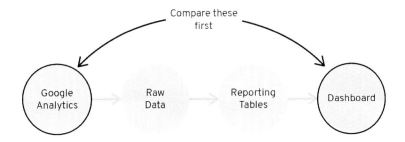

I may not have direct access to Google Analytics. Perhaps I don't have the necessary credentials. In that scenario, I check the dashboard against the raw data, since that's the earliest source of truth I can access directly.

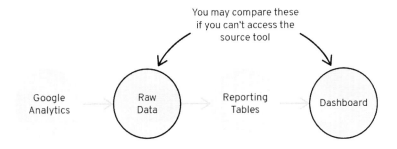

Checking against the earliest source of truth is the MOST important part of quality checking a data solution.

Data Duplication Does Not Occur

When you combine and manipulate data, it's extremely easy to duplicate rows. For example, you may want to calculate total profit for "Store 342." You pull that data from the accounting table. But you display the store's street name in your report, so you must join your data to a different store information table.

However, the store info table has two separate entries for Store 342 with unique addresses, because Store 342 closed and moved to a new location. So joining the two tables, without taking that into account, doubles the profit for Store 342 in your reporting.

Experienced data workers learn it's an easy mistake to make, but newer employees usually don't realize how often data duplication occurs.

A Leads to B Consistently

With most data solutions, common cause-and-effect actions occur when the data meets certain criteria.

For example, a report developer wants the number format on a dashboard's KPI boxes to change from "$1,000K" to "$1.0M" when the revenue goes over a million, just like expenses does in this screenshot.

Revenue	Expenses
$2,297.2K	$2.0M

Another example is when a database developer creates indicator fields using CASE statements. If they assign values based on specific logic, make sure it works as intended.

Math Is Correct

For reporting and database development, make sure the math is correct. If you want to calculate average profit per store, manually check that math by dividing the total profit and by total store count in a calculator or spreadsheet. This may sound pretty basic, but business intelligence tools don't always account for granularity as you expect.

Ironically, analysis projects have an easier time with ensuring the math is correct. R and Python have functions to calculate complicated statistical tests. You just have to use the right inputs.

Along the same lines, you must make sure your functions are appropriate for the data in question. For example, never take an average of averages (although true mathematicians will know the exception to this rule).

Generic Checklists

Below are generic quality checklists to get you started. Update them with common errors your team finds during quality checking tasks and adapt them to fit your line of work.

Quality Checklist for Database Developers

When checking a database, you should validate the following:
- Data matches the source system
- Schema matches the design specs
- Data sets provide fields specified on requirements document
- Primary key is included as a column
- Timestamp is included as a column
- Error logging is properly included
- Stored procedure / view logic is written efficiently

- Data duplication does not occur from joins
- *Select ** is never used
- Math is correct
- A leads to B

Quality Checklist for Report Developers

When checking a dashboard, you should validate the following:
- Data matches the source system
- Dashboard matches mockup and requirements doc
- Summary KPIs match other data points on dashboard
- Math is correct
- Padding, borders, and containers are consistent
- Tooltips show up as intended
- Fonts are used consistently
- Filters and parameters apply to the right metrics
- Spelling is accurate
- A leads to B

By the way, you can get a free guide on my website www.taylorrodgers.com illustrating how to check these items on a Tableau dashboard.

Quality Checklist for Analysis Projects

When quality checking analysis projects, you should validate the following:
- Data matches the source system
- Specified hypotheses were validated or rejected
- Math is correct
- Statistical tests are applied appropriately
- Data manipulation didn't distort data
- Only outliers from errors were excluded

- Spelling and grammar on presentation materials is correct

Things to Remember

- Quality checking is a simple process that improves stakeholder satisfaction
- Quality checking involves two people
- Quality checking is not a secondary responsibility, but a primary one
- The best quality checking process ensures:
    - Data matches earliest source tool available
    - Data duplication does not occur
    - A leads to B consistently
    - Math is correct
- Develop your own quality checklist to suit your needs

7

What Tools Are Used in Data Work?

When you build a data solution, your end product has more in common with an irrigation system than software. A data solution is meant to allow data to *flow* like water from one place to the other, eventually ending up in the hands of the end user.

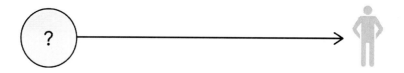

Seeing data solutions from this angle makes it much easier to understand how these tools work and why they're important. There are five types of tools you can use to improve the flow of data. Your team may use all five or specialize in one, including:

1. Data Source
2. Data Warehouse
3. ETL
4. Reporting
5. Analysis

Some tools have their own user interface and involve little-to-no programming. Some are simple programs or scripts that complete key tasks or display data. And others exist on a server that you'll seldom interact with directly.

Data Sources

The data source is the first tool type. These aren't really data tools, per se. Instead, they produce the data you want to use. Since I work in marketing, my common data sources are Facebook, Google Ads, and Google Analytics. Other common data sources include project management tools, CRMs, and accounting systems.

Data sources may also be programs your company builds. For example, online stock brokers like Charles Schwab and E-Trade probably have proprietary programs that generate data about customer trading activity.

Whatever the data source, both you and your team should become familiar with the user interface (UI). This enables quality checking the source directly and helps you understand how that impacts databases and reporting. For example, I'm quite familiar with Google Ads, despite never building a campaign in that platform. I'm comfortable working with it because I've logged in frequently to see exactly what my stakeholders see in the data.

Data Warehouse

The data warehouse is a platform or software that stores data in organized, structured databases and tables. The most common data warehouse tools use SQL, which stands for *Structured Query Language.*

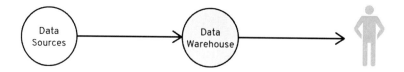

Some of these are cloud-based while others require your own internal servers. You will likely need help from a database or IT administrator for the initial setup and configuration.

Some common data warehouse tools include:

- Amazon Redshift
- Microsoft SQL Server
- mySQL
- Oracle Server
- PostgreSQL

ETL Tool

An ETL tool takes data from a data source and delivers it to the data warehouse. ETL stands for *extract, transform,* and *load.* It can also be used to manipulate data within a server. It's more complex than my simple description, but you need an ETL tool to populate any database with data existing outside the server.

More so than any other tool, limit yourself to one ETL tool. It's a harder skill to train and scarcer than report development. Granted, someone who knows SSIS can probably learn Oracle Data Integrator as well, but it's harder to find someone who already knows both. For the sake of simplicity, stick to one.

Many ETL tools exist out there. Some common ETL tools include:

- Microsoft SQL Server Integration Services (SSIS)
- Pentaho
- Oracle Data Integrator
- SAP Business Objects Data Services
- Alteryx

You can also build your own ETL programs using open-source programming languages, such as Python. They often have pre-built packages for common data sources like Google Analytics.

Reporting Tools

A reporting tool is how most end users see the data you want to deliver. A good reporting tool empowers you to deliver data in a fast, accessible, secure, and visually appealing way to less tech savvy users.

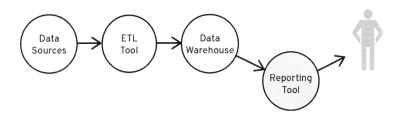

Reporting tools can usually only *read* data from the server. A select few can *write* data as well. Some tools are simple and easy to use, while others require a developer mindset.

Most data quality issues surface in the reporting tool. A common mistake is blaming the reporting tool for these issues, when they can happen at any point in the data flow chart above.

Some common reporting tools include:
- Tableau
- Domo
- PowerBI
- Google Data Studio
- Logi Analytics
- Microsoft SQL Server Reporting Services (SSRS)
- R Shiny Apps

Analysis Tools

Analysis tools offer the most flexibility when working with data. It's far easier to query data, manipulate it in the tool directly, and run a wide variety of statistical tests.

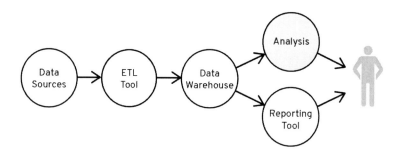

Some analysis tools are basically just a statistical programming language, such as R. Others are fully interactive tools, such as JMP. Some reporting tools, like Tableau, can produce visual analysis too.

You can also use *some* analysis tools to write data to your database. This makes sense when you build a model that needs to be referenced in a reporting tool or you build a machine learning program that needs to write results back to the database.

Common analysis tools and programming languages include:
- R
- Python
- JMP
- SAS
- Stata

Interactive Development Environments

Many of the tools listed earlier are standalone products. Others involve programs and programming languages. For the latter, you'll typically need an *Interactive Development Environment* or "IDE" for short.

IDEs exist *outside* the data flow process, but they allow data workers to interact and manage the programs and scripts within it.

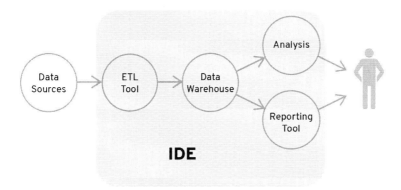

This is a subtle difference to make because many people consider IDEs as synonymous with many of the tools mentioned earlier. For example, RStudio is an IDE for the R programming language. Same with how Microsoft SQL Server Management Services is an IDE for Microsoft SQL Server.

Some common IDEs include:
- Aginity Workbench
- Microsoft SQL Server Management Services (SSMS)
- Oracle SQL Developer
- DBVisualizer
- Alation
- data.world
- Visual Basic
- RStudio
- JupyterLab
- JupyterNotebook

Notes on Excel and Google Sheets

You'll notice I haven't mentioned Excel or Google Sheets so far. That's because they are NOT business intelligence tools. And definitely NOT data science tools. Excel once had its place in reporting, but that time has long passed. Those still using it for reporting or analysis do so because they stick to what's comfortable, making their skillset woefully outdated. I'd personally never hire a data worker for a non-entry level position whose only skill was Excel.

Here are three big reasons why spreadsheet tools are not valid BI tools:

1. They don't scale well. The tools I mentioned previously are way more efficient and advanced. It's worth investing the time to learn one or more of them to improve your data solutions.
2. They are frequently used as band-aid solutions to common foundational data issues. These include key mapping, parameter updates, and rewriting past inputs.
3. They increase the risk of manual mistakes and decrease data accuracy. Quality declines significantly as you add more human inputs to a solution.

Things to Remember

- *Data sources* typically include their own BI tools and your team should familiarize with those user interfaces
- *Data warehouses* store your data for access by other tools
- *ETL tools* allow you to extract, transform, and load your data
- *Reporting tools* help you build visually appealing and accessible reports for less tech savvy end users
- *Analysis tools* run higher level statistical analysis on the data
- *IDEs* allow you to write and interact with the various programs in the data flow process
- Excel and Google Sheets are not valid BI tools

8

How to Hire and Onboard Data Workers

Demand is strong for data workers and supply is not keeping up. Industries that once cared little for data now actively recruit them. This imbalance in supply and demand makes a hiring manager's job far more difficult. A candidate with just a single year of SQL or Tableau experience gets frequent phone calls from recruiters. That means if you're interviewing them, someone else probably is too.

Employers Don't Have Power In Today's Job Market

During the Great Recession, employers could post a job opening and watch a rush of qualified candidates apply. I call this the **post-and-wait** approach to hiring.

In this environment, employers have all the power. Applicants have to work harder to convince employers to hire them. They must show more patience with the hiring process. Employers can require more testing to vet necessary skills and hold more power over salary negotiations.

That's not the case for data jobs today though. Those jobs are abundant in today's labor market. The demand for data workers is at an all-time high.

For some reason though, many employers still operate like they're in a job scarcity market. They think they can still just post and wait. Some do this out of habit since it always worked in the past. Others naively believe their company's reputation or "employer brand" does all the work for them.

Truth is applicants don't really care much about an employer brand. I've always thought that was a dubious concept anyways. Besides, companies with the best employer brands are usually just good employers in general.

What One Recruiter Says About Job Seekers

During my research, I interviewed Doug Washington. Doug is the Director of Recruiting Strategy for TriCom Technical Services, an IT staffing and recruiting firm.

I asked him what motivated people to leave one job for another.

"Money and location are always big," he said. "And location now also includes the ability to work remotely. So those two factors are always part of the decision. And no matter what any candidate ever says, they behave in a way where salary and location make a difference."

Research covered in later chapters supports his claim, adding one more key consideration – growth opportunities. If a candidate believes they will learn marketable skills or gain promotions, they're more enticed to work for you.

In shorter words, the three biggest motivations for someone to leave their job and work for you include:
1. Salary
2. Growth opportunities
3. Location (or option to work remotely)

You need to fulfill at least two of these motivations to attract high quality applicants. If you accomplish all three, you will attract the best talent and reduce turnover in the process. (I'll revisit turnover in more depth later on.)

In an ideal world, you have an unlimited hiring budget, all the time in the world to train and promote, and allow everyone the option to work from home. But that isn't always possible for you. Company rules or your own boss's opinion may prevent you from satisfying all three motivations.

Just recognize that these limitations impact the **type** of candidate you can attract and recruit.

The Two Types of Candidates

There's two types of candidates available to hire:
1. Experienced candidates who already have the skills you need
2. Aptitude candidates who don't have relevant work experience, but have potential to develop the skills you need

Both types of candidates prioritize different things in their job search. Experienced people prioritize salary and location. Aptitude candidates prioritize growth opportunities.

If you can compete on salary and location, you can hire for experience. If you can't compete on salary and location, you hire for aptitude and train that team member into what you need.

Hiring for Experience

Most companies want experienced candidates. They seem like safer bets, but still come with challenges.

First, they cost more. You can't hire an experienced, effective candidate with below market rates. So don't even try if you can't compete on salary.

Second, they are more likely to want to work remotely (at least part of the time) or want an office closer to home. That isn't true for everyone though. Some people, after working remotely long enough, miss basic human interaction and prefer to come to the office. I still recommend offering a remote work option though, for at least two days a week to stay competitive with other employers.

Lastly, these candidates are far less likely to apply directly to a job listing. You must actively reach out and recruit them. You may need a recruitment agency to help if you don't have time to do it yourself.

Experienced Employees Won't Put Up With Excessive Testing

It's prudent to test the technical skills of all job candidates, right? Sadly, it's just not feasible. The greatest irony is people most likely to pass technical tests are least likely to tolerate them. Experienced employees get so many recruiters calls that they're likely to get another job offer before completing your test.

Recruiter Doug Washington advises against too much testing. "Sometimes the reaction of a technologist is 'I don't want to take a test! These other jobs aren't making me take a test!'"

It's also difficult to test tech skills anyways. Most questions asked through testing software are more academic in nature and don't apply to real-world situations. Or the answers are easy to Google.

"It's like Goldilocks," said Doug. "Not too hot, not too cold. You got to have the right amount of testing. And that testing needs to give an indication of someone's technology skills. But there's not going to be a way to employ a single test that is both non-intrusive to not turn off the candidate and at the same time give you complete information on their skill level."

Companies with strong name recognition and a reputation for paying high salaries get away with more comprehensive testing. I knew an experienced and knowledgeable data scientist from my graduate program who went through weeks of interviewing, testing, and delivering a practice project. The company she applied for? Apple.

If you work for Apple or another prestigious tech company, you can get away with more rigorous testing. If you work for a smaller, less famous company, I recommend a simple test before or during the interview. For example, I once completed a written test in an interview where I marked up errors in a SQL script printed out in front of me. It was an elegantly simple test because someone with experience in SQL would immediately notice the errors without running the script on a computer. You can also set a computer in front of them and ask them to write a certain piece of code to perform a specific action.

Other Ways to Verify Skills Without Tests

One of the best things about data analytics is the community. Many data professionals enjoy sharing knowledge and doing side projects.

Tableau developers post Tableau dashboards built for fun on public.tableau.com. Data scientists use kaggle.com to practice algorithms on publicly available data. Others, like me, write articles.

Instead of requiring tests, simply ask job candidates about their side projects. Those projects exhibit certain sets of skills, which helps you determine if they possess the right technical aptitude and apply best practices in their work.

Ryan Sleeper, founder of PlayfairData and author of *Practical Tableau*, told me he uses Tableau Public's Gallery to determine if someone has the right technical skills to work for him. The best thing about Ryan's approach is how it demonstrates a candidate's real passion for the work, not just a list of skills on paper.

Experienced Employees Won't "Hit the Ground Running"

"Virtually every time we talk to a client," said Doug Washington, "they say 'I want somebody that can hit the ground running.' Well, there is no such thing."

Many hiring managers naively assume a more experienced hire produces positive results faster. That's true to a certain extent. You don't invest as much in training on key technical skills, but this benefit is somewhat exaggerated.

"Everybody needs ramp-up time," continued Doug. "It doesn't matter how experienced, how technologically in-depth somebody is, there's always a certain amount of ramp-up time."

I've never liked the "hit the ground running" phrase either. It sounds lazy to me. It offloads any responsibility for proactive onboarding to the employee.

As I discuss in later chapters on turnover, technical skills are interchangeable. Your architecture and business strategy are not. So even with a highly skilled database developer, they won't understand your database's hidden nuances right away. That must be learned, no matter the level of experience.

Experienced Employees Won't Always Deliver Higher Quality Work Than Inexperienced Employees

You likely get better results with more experience, but that's no guarantee. They possibly picked up bad habits at previous organizations and don't follow best practices discussed in this book, such as requirements gathering and quality checking.

If they were never required to consult with stakeholders or submit work for quality checking, their practical experience isn't worth as much. Now, if they adapt to the culture outlined previously, they'll be a great addition to your team. If they don't, I wouldn't obsess over them.

Inexperienced applicants actually have an advantage here. Since they're newer to the analytics world, they're more likely to accept your processes and work as a cohesive team. So it's possible an inexperienced employee's work quality quickly catches up to an experienced employee within a year.

Hiring For Aptitude

Hiring for aptitude means finding candidates with the intellectual capacity and demonstrated interest to do the job, but little to no relevant work experience.

With these candidates, you must evaluate educational background, how they ask and answer interview questions, and other personal experiences to determine fit for the role.

Aptitude candidates are appealing for a number of reasons. They have a clean slate and don't bring bad habits learned elsewhere to your team. They're also cheaper to hire, which is handy if you're on a budget.

Whereas experienced candidates prioritize salary and location, these candidates focus primarily on growth. Location is a moderate factor, but don't feel pressure to offer a remote work option. They need more in-person guidance anyways to get up to speed with this type of work.

Aptitude Candidates Require Training

While you save on upfront salary costs, these candidates require a higher training investment – both on process and technology.

Some training can be assigned self-study while other subjects require an actual class structure. You also need to pair them up with a more experienced mentor.

Aptitude Candidates Won't Be "Self-Starters"

The only phrase I dislike more than "hit the ground running" is "we only hire self-starters." The term "self-starter" is applied more to aptitude candidate hires than experienced hires.

Many managers state with confidence that they only hire self-starters, as if they're the "shrewd" and "no nonsense" type. They don't have the time to hold people's hands. They hire people who teach themselves how to get the job done.

This is not a proactive or supportive management approach though. You're doing both the employee and yourself a disservice by not training.

I'm a self-starter and have taught myself many skills, from Tableau to SQL to R. I believe I'm better than most at teaching myself new skills. However, past employers still waited a lot longer for me to deliver value while I taught myself how to perform many tasks. They could've generated more value, more quickly out of me with the right training investment.

Bootcamps Make Good Training

If you don't have the bandwidth or the right knowledge to train employees yourself, Doug Washington suggests bootcamps.

"There was an applicant that had a lot of the precursor skills and experience for the technology the client wanted him to have," he told me. "We asked 'what if we send that person to a boot camp?'"

Coding boot camps or training companies offer a way for employers to attract higher quality applicants without paying higher salaries. You pay for the training, secure a strong candidate, save on starting salary, and increase career advancement opportunities for them as well.

"This applicant didn't have the work experience they wanted," said Doug. "But we sent him to the boot camp and the guy has worked at the company for a year now – and doing fantastically!"

The employer got a productive employee, but there was another measurable benefit.

"The other advantage for the company," continued Doug. "Was that his salary was much lower than what they were expecting to pay for somebody with that particular experience."

Cost Comparisons of Experience versus Aptitude

To contrast the cost of hiring for experience versus aptitude, I'll use Tableau developers for example.

Depending on the market, an experienced Tableau developer costs between $75,000 to $90,000 a year. Sometimes higher.

An employee without relevant work experience but technical aptitude costs between $45,000 to $60,000.

A good third-party Tableau training program costs approximately $2,000.

You save approximately $30-43k hiring for aptitude and training them.

Don't Expect Loyalty From Aptitude Hires

We'll revisit in more depth later, but if you want to retain aptitude hires, you must offer annual raises to keep up with market rates. Otherwise they will leave.

Many employers naively assume because they gave an employee their first big break, they'll stick around without salary increases out of gratitude.

That's not how the real world works though. Working for you, aptitude hires will gain enough practical experience to start getting frequent recruiter phone calls. They may like you and your company personally, but it's still difficult to keep turning down a $10,000 raise from recruiters if you don't also keep up with their fair market value.

What Demonstrates Aptitude?

So how can you tell if someone has the aptitude for data work? If they have no relevant work experience, isn't it just a lucky guess?

Here are a few quick clues for analytics aptitude:

1. STEM education
2. Side projects
3. School projects
4. Technical training and certification

STEM Education

This one's easy. With a degree in statistics, economics, math, physics, engineering, computer science, or finance, they will easily learn business intelligence tools.

Let me clarify though – just because candidates don't have STEM degrees doesn't mean they won't do well. Some of the most talented data practitioners I know don't have STEM degrees. But skills taught in these majors naturally align with data work. So if you have no other way to determine aptitude, you can reduce the risk of a mis-hire using this criteria.

You can also check individual courses. Someone with a master's in public policy or sociology likely took upper-level stat classes, which likely involved programming in SAS or R as well. They could still provide value on your data team, even though the degree itself seems irrelevant.

Side Projects

Nothing's stopping an aptitude candidate from producing side projects like experienced candidates. They can produce work on Kaggle and Tableau Public as well. However, lower your expectations when reviewing this work. Their code or dashboards are a little rougher around the edges than more experienced candidates. Remember: you're not looking for perfection, but aptitude.

During the interview, ask them how they approached the project and worked through issues that cropped up. Give feedback on their work and see if they react positively, which exhibits humility and coachability

School Projects

If they pursued a data science or statistics degree, they probably produced an analysis project in class at some point. I did this for my master's program. Ask candidates to provide this analysis as part of their portfolio.

People without data science or statistics degrees likely produce other research projects that exhibit data skills. Most (good) research uses stats or data to a certain degree, which reveals how they gather and apply data to answer questions.

If the candidate produced projects in an undergraduate program, lower your evaluation standards. Undergraduates usually receive less mentorship than graduate students and their research projects reflect that. Grad students are usually older, with more real-world work experience and mentor guidance, so their projects should have a higher level of quality. Again, remember to look for aptitude here and not experience.

Training and Credentials

Some candidates do you a favor and get certified through a training program. This is a major aptitude signal. Use your judgement to determine the quality of certifications, but regardless, this still provides proof of two things:

1. They're serious enough to spend their own money on training
2. A third-party verifies they have the foundational skills to get started

You can also proactively reach out directly to training programs and let them know you're hiring. They can direct their students to apply.

Recruiter Doug Washington is a big fan of these programs. "I think companies need to be a lot more open to hiring people coming through a bootcamp. They're often even better than hiring someone right out of college."

Why? Many people attend technical bootcamps because they already have one career and they're looking to start a new one.

"That person will often have an established work history," said Doug. "So they understand what it's like to be an employee and show up to work and get along with other people."

Salary Negotiations

I explore salary and why it matters in more detail later, but I'll briefly comment on negotiations here. The best policy is to offer a fair market salary and transparently share how you decided that offer. If you use payscale.com, tell them. They'll feel like the salary is determined fairly.

Keep in mind it's illegal in many cities and states to ask someone their current salary. It's also illegal in many places to tell employees they can't discuss salaries with coworkers. One of my previous employer's executives regularly coached new hires on "professional behavior." That included not discussing salary with co-workers, which was an illegal suggestion. Unsurprisingly, that company gets sued frequently. I received two separate settlement checks from class action lawsuits because disgruntled employees sued them for these labor violations.

Such laws mean you shouldn't attempt to "win" salary negotiations as an employer. Be honest and transparent. If you win in the short-term and successfully convince a candidate to accept below market salary, the employee will find out eventually they're underpaid. And they'll be more likely to leave you after a year or so when a recruiter calls with a higher offer.

If you're worried you'll get too far in a job offer only to discover you can't compete on salary, you may ask ahead of time what the candidate expects for compensation.

If a candidate states a seemingly high number, don't write them off too quickly. Merely counter with your own market estimate and ask to compare with their research. They may be asking for way more than the actual market rate as a negotiation tactic. Counter such behavior with data.

Job Posting

Writing a job post is remarkably similar to writing any internet advertisement. Plain English works better. Clearly state the job needs and benefits. Avoid business jargon and fluff.

Be Careful With Technical Requirements in a Job Opening

Every once in awhile, I see a job opening like this, "We require five years experience in R, T-SQL, NoSQL, Python, Java, JavaScript, SAS, Powershell, .NET, and C#." While some people may know all ten of those programming languages, I doubt they're proficient in all of them. Also, this sounds like multiple jobs and the hiring manager thinks they can make one person do all of them.

Recruitment agencies tend to discourage excessive technical requirements. Not because they make hiring harder. They just make it unrealistic altogether. It also discourages high aptitude applicants because they assume they're unqualified if they don't meet every requirement.

One recruitment company hired me for a job that originally required both SSIS and SSRS. I only had SSRS experience, but they found another guy with SSIS experience. They recommended the employer hire us both as specialists rather than generalists because it's hard to find people who know both tools with high proficiency.

In addition to unrealistic technical requirements, be careful requiring experience with certain versions of software.

Doug Washington said too many companies disregard applicants over which software version they used last.

"They want this person to have experience with version six of this particular technology and the candidate has version five. And I'll ask the client, 'So what's the difference between version five and version six?' The client doesn't even know."

Software usually doesn't change much from one version to the next. Some exceptions exist of course, but someone who last used Tableau 2018 can easily translate those skills to Tableau 2020.

Don't Make a Fool of Yourself With Software Requirements

Many hilarious examples exist online of job ads stating something like, "We want 10 years of experience in X programming language," when X programming language was only invented 5 years ago. One guy actually invented a programming language, then applied for a job requiring that same language as a skill. He was denied because he had too few years of experience. He took a screenshot and posted it on the internet.

Job Posting Websites

Don't use complex application systems where applicants must retype their whole resume. It wastes the applicant's time and deters many candidates from even applying. Instead, use websites like ZipRecruiter or LinkedIn that easily import work history.

Both sites feature an "easy apply" option where applicants apply with a few clicks. Since resumes are already in their LinkedIn profile (or in a PDF on ZipRecruiter), you reduce hassle for qualified people.

Onboarding

Nothing's worse than starting a job and not knowing what to do. And then finding out your manager is constantly in meetings your first week. Develop a game plan to get an employee successfully started on the job. And one that's more than just getting them a computer and an email account.

Jared Sloan, Vice President of Data Solutions at Alight Analytics, suggests an onboarding schedule. "These are extremely helpful for new people that come in on a team," he said. "Like alright, these are exactly the things you need to learn in the first 30 days. This is exactly what I expect you to learn in 60 and 90 days."

We'll delve deeper into job role clarity in the next chapter, but this is a great way to define expectations for success ahead of time. Employees love it too.

Contract-to-Hire

Jared Sloan lets people go if they don't meet expectations in an onboarding plan. That's common practice in many environments. If you feel guilty about hiring someone only to possibly fire them later, try the contract-to-hire approach.

The contractor takes the job knowing there's less security if they don't meet expectations. This also allows them to retain their dignity in future job searches since they didn't get fired – they just finished a contract.

Things to Remember

- You can't fight the labor market
- Salary, location, and growth are the three biggest motivators for job candidates
- Experience hires care more about salary and location
- Aptitude hires care more about growth opportunities
- Training aptitude hires is the cost of paying lower salaries
- STEM majors, side projects, school projects, technical credentials, published blogs or articles, and public speeches are better ways to evaluate experience and aptitude than traditional testing
- Use an onboarding schedule

9

Managing, Motivating, and Retaining Data Workers

At the start of this book, I said managers should focus attention on continuous outcomes. That's especially true with your employees. Hiring, training, retention, and satisfaction are all continuous outcomes you impact directly. Along with quality, they're the strongest reflection of management performance – both for the direct supervisor and the company as a whole.

Many might say it's all situational and there's no magic formula to improving these outcomes. That's simply not true. It is situational, but as a manager, even without much institutional authority, you can improve these outcomes.

You might ask if such simple solutions exist, why are there so many unhappy employees with bad managers?

Bad Managers Aren't Proactive in Managing

Managers and executives take either **passive** or **reactive** approaches to management. That partly comes from the nature of corporations. Responsibility for improving employee success is diluted when more and more people get the "manager" title. Decisions regarding promotions, growth opportunities, and salary ranges become a committee decision rather than the decision of a single person.

A reactive approach also attempts to minimize risk. Some managers don't want to rock the boat by clearly communicating policies and solutions to common problems. They worry about how their employees or their own boss will react. If something is made clear, then any issues with it are also clear, potentially introducing reputational risk. So managers and executives wait too long to address small issues like salary expectations until they become too big to fix and a valuable employee leaves.

My approach is different. I say be **proactive** in fixing common problems **before** they ever become problems. That's my first big theme for this chapter: proactively plan and implement to preempt future problems.

Proactivity Is Useless Without Communication

My second big theme is to be open, straightforward, and *respectful* in your communication. This connects to the implementation part. Many people are smart enough to see how the world works and ways to improve it, but they lack the communication skills to rally their teams around solutions.

You must be open to establish trust. Employees aren't clueless to what you're thinking. They can tell when you withhold information. Many managers hold back because of personal insecurity or fear of what employees might do with such information. This clearly isn't proactive however.

Straightforwardness reduces ambiguity and encourages employees to buy into your vision. That's true of company policies, career growth opportunities, and performance improvement. None of those areas are effective without straightforward communication.

Respectfulness is the most critical factor many people miss unfortunately. I've met many straightforward people who take that openness as a license to be disrespectful or condescending. Their "honesty" has the opposite effect of what's needed because it turns people off. If this rings true for you, you might say that's just the way it is and other people should adapt. As a manager though, your behavior is not your team's problem, it's **yours**. If the ten people working with you have certain expectations of behavior, you must adapt or move on.

Employees Won't Always Tell You What They Want

Before adapting your approach, understand what employees want. Get to know them and do your own research. You can't rely on employees directly stating what they want because they may worry such honesty might backfire.

When I first took over managing my team, I sent a list of questions to get to know them. The questions asked about preferred communication and feedback style, professional goals, motivations, and more. One question asked if they viewed the company as a stepping stone to another opportunity. Another question asked if their goal was to become a more talented Tableau Developer or did they have other career goals afterwards. I was fine with any answer because it helped me help them achieve their goals in the most direct way possible.

Every team member said they wanted to stay with the company and just get good in their current role. Some told the truth, while others did not. I don't think they "lied" in the unethical sense, but they held back some "personal truth," not wanting to give a bad impression. As I got to know them, I learned their initial answers weren't entirely true in all cases. Some wanted to pursue data science, move internally within the company, and one really did want to become a Tableau Zen Master.

Employees withhold this info because they were probably burned by a bad boss previously or warned by parents or professors about what not to tell a boss. Like many managers, they're minimizing the risk of your reactions and subsequent actions against them.

You can chip away at this hesitation over time by being open and honest yourself and not punishing them for being the same with you. That takes time but the investment is worth it.

Manage and Motivate Employees By Assuming the Average

Since you're reading this book, I suspect we're kindred spirits. You probably go to great lengths to actively manage your career, learn new technical skills to advance, and read every book out there to help navigate complex corporate politics. That focus on personal growth probably served you well and helped you land your current position. But there's a common tendency for people like us to assume most others share those same traits.

I think it's better to take the opposite position. Most workers are, by definition, average or within range of average. You can't hire a full team of only top performers and self-starters. I hear all the time, "We only hire the best." While that's technically possible, it's statistically not likely. Only one person in your profession is the "best" at their job. Exclusively hiring only the "best" people takes one helluva hiring budget and sales pitch.

By acknowledging most employees are within average, you can build processes, training, and culture that boosts performance of average employees and dramatically increases performance of top performers.

Fret not though. You're not doomed to accept apathetic and dimwitted employees. The average person in data work has higher intellect than people in many other professions. I used to think I was the smartest person ever. Humble, right? Then I started working with other people in the analytics field. That's when I learned, to my horror, that I'm average afterall.

I'll even go as far to say data workers have higher interest in career advancement and growth than people in other professions. That might relate to age since they tend to be younger.

That said, the wants and needs of data workers aren't all that different from employees in any other industry.

What Employees Want: Define Expectations and Success in Their Current Role

People don't like ambiguity on what you expect them to do. If ambiguity exists, you failed your managerial responsibility to proactively define and communicate expectations. And just saying "work hard and have a good attitude" doesn't cut it either.

If your company historically offers promotions to "Lead" or "Sr." titles, clearly define how to move up to these positions. Someone on my team once asked how they could get the "Sr." title for their current role. Another person received that promotion before I arrived, but the company had no set policy for it. Turns out that promotion was awarded for taking on a very large and complicated project.

I'm personally not a fan of "Sr." and "Lead" titles. They create an unnecessary hierarchy and cause co-workers to compare themselves to one another. Sometimes it even leads to outright resentment.

But that company set a precedent for the Sr. title and now the entire staff wanted it. Go figure. I didn't have an answer when my direct report asked about it. I could've taken a reactive approach, making something up on the spot. I could've used her question as a carrot to influence her to change things about herself. But I didn't do any of those things.

Instead, I told her I didn't have an answer and I'd get back to her. I didn't want to react impulsively. I took some time and attempted to define success for her role. I made sure it wasn't specific to her or anyone else.

Next time we discussed it, I handed her a three-page document clearly explaining success in her role. I loved her expression, "My gosh! This is detailed!"

Defining success by role also reduces your bias against your own team. I'm not being politically correct here. People tend to hire and promote those with similar personalities, opinions, and other shared traits.

When you proactively define success for your team roles, employees can easily adapt approaches and behaviors to meet expectations. You also safeguard against your own bias or personal views about the employees. Performance evaluation becomes more objective and fair for the team and easier for you as a manager.

What Employees Want: Promotion for Success in Current Role

Employees want to be promoted for succeeding in their current role. If you define the path to Sr. or Lead clearly, you must follow through when they meet those goals. Now I can hear some people saying, "W-Wait! You're saying I have to promote and give raises for my entire team if they're all performing the way I want them?!"

Yes! When you clearly define what employees must do to succeed, and they do it, you have to follow through! And why wouldn't you? Productivity has improved! That deserves recognition and reward!

What Employees Want: The Chance to Modify the Role

There's a trade off to defining role expectations and success. Every person is unique with a different set of strengths. For some, becoming more proficient in a role and getting the "Sr."

title is enough. For others, they see a role as a stepping stone to another position, such as data scientist or data strategist. I worked with one person who didn't want promotions. She wanted to move through a variety of departments because she liked learning new things.

There are ways to handle such workplace nomads, but it's trickier if your teams require specialization. One of my previous companies had such a high volume of data work, it required separate teams for database developers, data scientists, web analysts, and report developers. We could not efficiently share those responsibilities across teams. That meant that my team (the reporting team) only built reports. They didn't write code or do statistics or machine learning. That can feel limiting for some.

Since increased specialization limits the available variety of work, find ways for your team to develop skills that allow them to transition if desired.

You can offer *al la carte* responsibilities for team members, which they pick based on career interests and strengths. If a strong communicator wants to develop into a leader or manager, they can lead the onboarding process and mentor new hires. If they want to become a strategist, they need to develop new process ideas and sell them through. If they want to become a data scientist, encourage them to incorporate statistics and higher-level analysis into their current report development activities.

I like the *al la carte* method, but Jared Sloan, Vice President of Data Solutions at Alight Analytics, had a different method that feels more organic. He defines a role, and also asks the employee how they'd define the role.

"You probably have clear career goals and I have an idea about where I want the team to go," he said. "Your opinion of what it is to be an analyst or database developer – we probably need to be able to customize that. These are people who have their own stuff to accomplish. If you don't do that, they're gonna get unhappy and leave and it sucks to hire new people in this field."

Whatever you do though, don't tell your employees, "Find opportunities on your own to do that in your role." Not defining a role's boundaries is frustrating. I've had jobs where I heard phrases like "find those opportunities" and spent a lot of time developing solutions, only to then hear I'm stepping on other people's toes. If you don't know the boundaries, work with your employees and other teams to find out where they are.

Some people don't like establishing boundaries thinking it limits initiative. But boundaries can actually offer pathways to overcome them. If an ETL developer wants to learn report development executed by a different team, they could become a backup report developer for that team. Employee satisfaction is fundamentally about discussing employee goals and finding overlap with organizational goals.

What Employees Want: Training

As covered before, training is important to keep employees at your company. The better the training, the less focus employees put on salary.

Poor or little training actually incentivizes employees to leave as well. One study found that 40% of employees who received poor training left their job within a year.[1]

Sadly, many managers neglect training in favor of hiring "self-starters." They want people who teach themselves the skills needed to succeed.

Neglecting training is not proactive management though. Even the best employees, true self-starters, cannot actually succeed

---

[1] Employee Training is Worth the Investment: ROI of Training: Tourism Info. (2020, March 03). Retrieved July 28, 2020, from https://www.go2hr.ca/training-development/employee-training-is-worth-the-investment

that way. You can dramatically shorten the time span self-starters need to become top performers with training. You also improve the performance of average employees by a lot too.

Training also effectively improves employee habits. Teach new processes, design standards, and technology via training. And it's especially critical and beneficial to train new employees to get them off on the right foot, as discussed in the last chapter.

What Employees Want: Better Training

Many managers think they train people when they really don't. Training should be as thorough and high quality as the products and services you expect employees to produce for your client.

The way you train is actually fairly straightforward:
- Explain the why of the activity
- Illustrate the concept
- Allow them to perform the action under your supervision
- Immediately follow up on the action to give feedback
- Provide documentation for them to reference later
- For the first few weeks, follow up occasionally

When I managed a team of Tableau developers, I thoroughly explained our process and how to QA dashboards to new employees. I relied on Tableau's online videos for teaching the technical side of Tableau. We also reviewed existing designs to walk through how they're built. For the first few weeks, I checked their dashboards using the same list I trained them on. I followed up immediately, offering guidance to improve performance. I was always available for questions. You can also ask more experienced employees to serve as mentors during this process.

For requirements gathering, which is far more challenging to teach, I built requirements for them and allowed them to shadow on requirements meetings until they felt comfortable taking over those meetings.

You don't have to personally develop all training though. As mentioned in the last chapter, boot camps and training consultants can also teach necessary skills and supplement internal training. This doesn't have to happen during the onboarding process either. Skill development and training is an ongoing process for employees.

Nick Stevens, Chief Data Officer of the University of Kansas, pays for speakers to visit his office to teach his staff new things. Instead of sending two people to a conference, he pays the same amount for a speaker to speak to his whole organization.

What Employees Want: Autonomy

Newer employees crave training and guidance. Experienced employees crave autonomy and respect. They want freedom to exercise their own judgement in their craft and your confidence in them. Micromanaging their code or dashboard discourages their efforts.

Granting more autonomy also increases job satisfaction and decreases the likelihood an employee will leave.[2]

You might think my stance on autonomy contradicts the rest of this book's advice. Since this book focuses on increasing operational efficiency, detailing processes, and defining role expectations, there's seemingly little room for autonomy. But that's actually not true.

My processes actually allow greater autonomy within requirements gathering, solution development, and data analysis. You're merely improving the business ecosystem, enabling your

---

[2] Blossom Yen-Ju Lin, Yung-Kai Lin, Cheng-Chieh Lin, Tien-Tse Lin, Job autonomy, its predispositions and its relation to work outcomes in community health centers in Taiwan, *Health Promotion International*, Volume 28, Issue 2, June 2013, Pages 166–177, https://doi.org/10.1093/heapro/dar091

top performers to do higher quality work in a more streamlined fashion. In this way, structure actually supports autonomy.

What Employees Want: More Productive Team Meetings

More often than not, weekly team meetings waste time, hamper productivity, and don't lead to significant improvement. Many managers use team meetings for project updates, but those updates don't provide value to co-workers not on those projects.

The best team meetings serve one of the following functions:
1. Improve team culture
2. Train the team on best practices
3. Solicit opinions on team direction from the team themselves
4. Provide company or strategy updates
5. Review mini internal case studies
6. Transfer knowledge on new tools, functionalities, or techniques

In my team meetings, I liked exploring deep-dive topics. They were always work related, expanding on a topic my team would find useful. I covered statistical concepts, new data sources, giving better presentations, and more. Anything that could improve the team and provide a benefit to all in attendance.

I also encouraged my direct reports to contribute to team meetings. Your team has talents you lack, and allowing them to share best practices makes team meetings more fun and engaging for everyone involved. For example, one of my employees taught the team about Facebook's various data points. Shine the spotlight on each of your employees in team meetings, rather than just yourself.

What Employees Want: More Money!

Most employees want money. That's obvious. Pay is cited as the biggest reason people look for new jobs.[3] They want to make as much money as possible. They'll visit Glassdoor.com, see their role's top tier makes $120k a year, and naturally assume they deserve the same.

I explore this more in the next chapter because employers, and sometimes even employees, are in denial about the importance of pay.

A Note on Retention

Everything I mention in this chapter is important for reducing employees' excuses for leaving. In the next chapter, I go into way more detail about how salary affects turnover. Creating a happy and engaging environment is important, but truly reducing turnover takes a radical approach most employers can't stomach.

Things to Remember

- Proactively fix the biggest complaints employees cite as reasons to leave a company
- Trust research to understand common complaints since most employees won't tell you directly
- Most employees have a unique set of talents, but their wants and needs are usually pretty universal
- Employees most commonly want the following:
    - Clear expectations and path to success in their

---

[3] Employee Retention: What Makes Employees Stay or Leave. (2016, August 19). Retrieved July 28, 2020, from https://www.paychex.com/articles/human-resources/employee-retention-what-makes-employees-stay-leave

role
- Promotion for succeeding in their current role
- Some flexibility in modifying role responsibilities
- Good training
- More autonomy
- More productive meetings
- More money

10

Salary Is More Important Than You Think (And Why It Indirectly Affects Quality)

In the first chapter, I said data quality is the foundation of success for data solutions and data teams. That means data quality is the ultimate reflection on whether a manager is succeeding in his or her role since data quality is impacted by the quality of operations.

One of the biggest factors in reducing data quality issues is **reducing turnover.**

Complexity and nuance abounds in any company's data. As a person gains experience, it's easier to learn new databases more quickly. But there's a limit. The history and 'gotcha' moments embedded in company data are not always intuitive, even to the most experienced workers.

Since ignorance about existing database and report architecture hampers accurate data delivery, managers must proactively tackle this huge issue. When an employee leaves, they take that institutional knowledge with them. One person's departure is salvageable, but multiple departures are devastating.

Outside of building good habits and quality-focused processes, reducing turnover is the biggest impact managers make on data quality. And what impacts an employee's decision to leave the most? **Money**.

Salary Is Not an Expense

I once attended a talk by Chet Cadieux, CEO of QuikTrip. I previously worked for the company and I enjoyed his talk to KU's business school about QuikTrip's "employee first" philosophy. One statement stuck with me over the years: "Accountants think of employees as expenses, but QuikTrip thinks of them as assets."

This wasn't just talk either. I made more working at QuikTrip than my first professional job out of college and almost as much as the second.

The salary you pay a data worker is an investment in their growing institutional knowledge about your company and your data. If they leave, so does that knowledge and investment.

Technical Skills Are Interchangeable – Your Architecture Is Not

It's not overly difficult to find or train new employees on SQL and Tableau. The real challenge is that every company and every database is unique. It takes about a year to fully understand a company's strategy and architecture. That's super important since data's purpose is to deliver accurate, actionable insights.

Let's run through a real-world example.

You have an employee making $60,000 a year. They walk in and say they want a $15,000 raise. A recruiter offered them $75,000 a year to do the exact same job at another company.

This seems like a huge raise. One that's usually reserved as a reward for good performance. You may feel it's not deserved either.

But let's consider another fact. The cost of replacing an employee is estimated at 21% of their yearly salary[4]. So the cost

---

[4] Boushey, H., & Glynn, S. J. (2012, November 16). There Are Significant Business Costs to Replacing Employees. Retrieved July 28, 2020, from

to replace an employee earning $60,000 is $12,600.

Now $12,600 is less than $15,000 a year. So it seems like it's cheaper to let that employee go.

But remember this: the employee wants a raise to the **market rate** of $75,000. That's their competing offer.

That means hiring an equally skilled employee would cost around $75,000 a year. And 21% of $75,000 is $15,750.

Now you might say that's only a $750 loss. But you're actually paying two costs.

First, the cost of paying an additional $15,000 a year to hire a new employee at the new market rate. The second is the estimated $15,750 in lost productivity.

Add those two numbers up and your actual cost is $30,750!

That's way more than the $15,000 your current employee wants. And remember: you have no guarantee the new hire will perform better than your current employee.

But Shouldn't My Employees Be Loyal?

Some business executives preach the importance of loyalty. They only want loyal employees who show gratitude by sticking around, even at lower salaries.

Those managers need to learn a harsh reality – an employee doesn't owe you anything for being hired. They express gratitude by performing their job duties. You express gratitude by paying them. The same as any other exchange of goods and services.

And why shouldn't your employees behave so? If you have two clients and limited resources, which client do you prioritize more? Probably the one who pays more, right? You cannot expect

---

https://www.americanprogress.org/issues/economy/reports/2012/11/16/44464/there-are-significant-business-costs-to-replacing-employees/

different behavior from employees. Their careers are, in a sense, their business.

You *earn* loyalty through fair pay and treating them as outlined in the last chapter. Then they stop seeing the job less as a transaction and more as a relationship.

But Don't Most Employees Leave For a Reason Other Than Pay?

A lot of managers repeat the phrase, "People leave because of poor managers, not for higher pay." Yes, a terrible boss makes many people leave, even if they pay well. That doesn't automatically mean employees who like you will stay with less pay though.

Doug Washington, Tri-Com Technical Services' Director of Recruiting Strategy, cautions employers not to downplay the importance of salary.

"If they have a bad boss or a bad manager," he said, "That's absolutely a factor. But we see people all the time say 'I love my job. Love it! Everything's great. Don't want to leave!' Six weeks later, they're in a new job and it's not because anything changed with their boss."

This isn't just Doug's personal experience. The data backs this up too. Payscale found that money was the primary reason someone *quit* their job.[5]

A Gallup[6] poll also identified the following as the two biggest reasons people quit jobs:

---

[5] Why Do People Quit Their Jobs? It's More Than Money. (n.d.). Retrieved July 28, 2020, from
https://www.payscale.com/data/why-people-quit-their-jobs
[6] Robison, J. (2020, February 06). Turning Around Employee Turnover. Retrieved July 28, 2020, from
https://news.gallup.com/businessjournal/106912/turning-around-yo ur-turnover-problem.aspx

1. Lack of career advancement and growth opportunities (32%)
2. Pay (22%)

These two data points probably look familiar. I mentioned them earlier in the chapter on hiring. I said experienced hires often leave a job if you can't offer them higher salaries and that aptitude hires prioritize growth opportunities more.

So, can you get away with not paying people more if you offer growth opportunities?

The answer is maybe.

Consider why aptitude hires prioritize growth opportunities. They believe growth opportunities bring higher salaries later. And once you fulfill their need for professional growth, salary quickly becomes the bigger motivator.

So you can get people in the door with growth opportunities, but getting them to stay requires salary raises.

You Will Run Out of Growth Opportunities

Not every employee gets a promotion into management and not every employee moves beyond the Sr. position. Some employees enjoy staying in one role and not seeking new educational opportunities. So the additional knowledge you offer has a marginal rate of return. If they already know how to build an ETL process, and that's all they want to do, does Tableau training benefit them or their career?

If the answer is no, then they will become increasingly motivated by money rather than growth opportunities.

For that reason, you can't make up for lower pay by providing a continuous stream of training. Learning opportunities lose their appeal and perceived value for many employees over time.

But Won't Young Workers Stay for 'Meaningful' Work?

In my first job's orientation, an older executive told a room full of millennials how they ("millennials") were willing to trade higher salaries in exchange for more meaningful and fulfilling work. He had "evidence" to back up the claim. And he's not completely wrong. Many millennials (or any young employee) do say things like that.

The problem is young people say a lot of things they *think* they mean. But then reality sets in. They start to have babies who need care and feeding. They have to pay off those student loans from college. They want to buy a home in their expensive dream city. Some marry and their spouse wants to work less or stay at home with children. Their own parents may need financial support. Life's realities mean that young people (and every future generation) *need* increasing amounts of money, and they'll pursue higher paychecks over meaningful work.

In shorter words, young workers idealistically describe the work they *want* to do, but realistically pursue other motivators in the work they *actually* do.

Your Company's Services Probably Aren't Meaningful to Young Workers

Some young workers may take lower paying jobs if they find the work meaningful, but they probably don't find your company's services meaningful – even if you do.

I've worked in healthcare, senior living, and marketing. Healthcare and senior living industries try to sell young workers on meaningfulness, but both companies were for profit and charged lots of money for their services. Their objective was making money, and employees were so far removed from people in need that any pretense of making a difference was lost on them.

When young workers say they want meaningful work, they probably mean reducing poverty, feeding the poor, supporting political causes, volunteering at church, etc. That feels like making a difference to them. Your company probably doesn't do any of those things in a significant way to make your employees' work feel meaningful.

And most young workers quickly realize meaningful work is not enough to pay for the lifestyle they or their families want.

Gender Also Factors into Meaningful Work Motivation

The idea that younger workers prioritize meaningful work also skews by gender. Pew found men and women, for the most part, value the same things in a job. However, 24% of women say having a job that helps society is extremely important, compared to 19% of men. That difference is more pronounced for millennials. 29% of millennial women, compared to 19% of millennial men, say a job that helps society is extremely important.[7]

I have anecdotal evidence to back this up as well. I majored in economics in college. The class was full of men wanting to work in finance, insurance, or some other high-paying analytical role. I took a liberal arts class in sociology, and it was full of women. They wanted to work for non-profits or the government, helping others.

Keep this in mind because typically more men than women work in data work. That means fewer employees or applicants are swayed by the meaningful work pitch. And I've also found

---

[7] Chapter 3: What Men, Women Value in a Job. (2019, December 31). Retrieved July 28, 2020, from https://www.pewsocialtrends.org/2013/12/11/chapter-3-what-men-women-value-in-a-job/

women in this field are equally as motivated as men by money and career advancement.

Young Workers Are Actively Encouraged to Job Hop

Young workers also get a very clear message from financial advice content targeted towards them – *job hop to get a raise.* Since many employers don't give raises based on accumulating years of experience, young workers feel they must move jobs every two to three years to increase wages to the market rate. Young workers who switch jobs frequently increase earnings and responsibilities at a far faster rate than young workers who don't. And this trend is even more pronounced for data workers with experience in SQL and other analytics tools.

Keep in mind, I'm not making a moral judgement on whether job hopping is a good thing or not. I'm just stating a fact – job hopping leads to more career advancement and income for young workers.

So Money Is Important – What Do I Do?

At a minimum, pay the **market rate**, unless your other benefits effectively make up for less salary. If I had an unlimited budget, I'd pay 10% above median wage for every role, because I want to attract quality and make it difficult for an employee to find a better offer.

But that poses a problem. I previously mentioned most employees think they're top performers. So they still think they're underpaid, even if they're slightly overpaid. Thankfully, there's a simple solution.

Make It Clear How You Determine Salary and Publicize the Salary Ranges for Job Roles

Define salary expectations per role and put them in your company documentation. If your salary policy follows what Payscale.com reports as the market rate, clearly state so and share that info with employees. When you offer a promotion to an employee, tell them the raise they can expect ahead of time.

This has many benefits, including:

1. Employees won't worry less experienced co-workers make more than them
2. Salary negotiations (which can work against you) become a non-issue

Research shows that more transparency about salary determination reduces feelings of unfairness among employees.

Provide Raises Based on Market Rate of Years of Experience

You can't just pay the market rate when you hire someone. You also must provide a clear expectation of raises to the market rate every year. If the market rate for an employee with five years experience was $55,000 and the following year it increases to $60,000, then the employee should get a minimum $5,000 raise.

Why should you do this? Well, if your employee is mid-20s to 30s (and many are in this profession), they'll probably leave to get that raise elsewhere. Remember: young workers are actively encouraged to job hop to get fair market wages.

You can reduce turnover by simply raising wages based on accumulated experience.

You might say that's an expensive policy, but remember – it's the *market rate*. To get another equally qualified candidate, you'll pay that amount to replace them and the *cost of training* a new hire.

So I Have to Give Raises Every Year?

Nope. Salaries for most roles peak at a certain point. It's perfectly fine to say, "You're maxed out. We can only give a cost of living raise." If you're paying the market rate, they likely won't find a better option elsewhere. It might also prompt them to consider a new higher salary role at your company, if money is their driving factor.

What If I Don't Have the Budget for Continual Raises?

Then get really good at fulfilling the other reasons employees stick around, like training, growth opportunities, and promotions. Tell them if they stay, they will learn such-and-such skills, which will make them more marketable, and will eventually get them a higher salary elsewhere. Just don't be surprised when they leave for that higher salary and don't judge them for doing so.

Use a Dual Strategy If You Have a Tight Budget

Another approach is continually investing in a handful of experienced employees and incentivise them to stay over time. That way you maintain a solid foundation of talent with institutional knowledge.

Then build a stellar training program and keep hiring less-experienced employees, expecting they'll probably leave you for higher salaries eventually.

Younger employees will view your company as a starter job or a place to gain new skills. Experienced employees view it as a place to stay long term.

For this approach to work, you must excel at onboarding, training, and mentoring them for the duration of their time with your company.

This strategy doesn't work for *all* employees though. Quality is critical to your success, and quality depends on qualified people knowing your data and architecture. So find ways to incentivize and keep a core group of experienced employees at the very least.

Salaries Don't Differ Much Across Regions Now

Many employers still operate as if individual job markets have different salary ranges. In other words, they say west coast salaries are different from midwest salaries.

According to Doug Washington, you shouldn't assume that anymore.

"You're seeing a nationalization of compensation levels," he said. "We used to have big differences between the coasts and the midwest because of the cost of living. With the exception of housing, cost of living has evened out across the country."

Since more companies allow remote work and cost of living is more consistent, salary levels are evening out across the country as well.

"If you're in Silicon Valley and people can work remotely," Doug continued. "You can hire people in Cincinnati, Ohio or Kansas City, Missouri or wherever. They can work remotely. We've seen that even out [compensation] a little bit nationally."

Salaries Differ Even Less *Within* States Too

Some employers complain they can't hire talent because their city has a lower salary rate than the next city over. For example, I live in a town called Lawrence. Kansas City is a 45-minute drive east and Topeka is a 35-minute drive west. I've heard employers state there's a compensation difference between the two markets.

The unavoidable reality is a smaller city close to a major city is in the same job market, whether you like it or not.

"We have several clients in Topeka, Kansas," said Doug. "They say this [salary level] is the norm for their market, but Topeka does not have the labor pool to fill those jobs. If you want to get people to come from Kansas City, who are going to have to commute five days a week, then you will have to pay Kansas City wages. You can't fight gravity."

What If My Top Performer Expects a Higher Salary than the Market Rate?

I think *top performer* is a subjective term. One company's top performer is another company's troublemaker. That said, one team member probably produces more value than others on a regular basis.

I stand by my statement that you should pay consistent salaries based on job titles and years of experience. But you can reward your high performer in other ways, if they want more than the market rate.

First, promote them or offer them a new role. Top performers are much more motivated by learning and open to change than typical employees.

Second, pay bonuses. Just because you match market rate salaries doesn't mean you have to limit financial bonuses.

Third, which you may or may not have the power to do, give an ownership stake. These are rare outside of management, but if you own your company, you can offer this to keep top talent.

Things to Remember

- Invest in quality and institutional knowledge by increasing salary
- Employees are investments, not costs
- Despite popular stereotypes, young workers are motivated by money and will job hop to earn more
- Clearly communicate how you determine salaries and what expected salaries are by role
- If you're on a limited budget, invest in a few key employees for the long term and focus on training lower-pay employees
- Reward top performers with bonuses or new opportunities instead of above-market salary increases

11

Types of Job Roles in Data Work

A lot of roles exist in data work. People debate their definitions relentlessly and get carried away with what each role should or shouldn't do. It doesn't help that each role can also carry a prestige or stigma with it. Keep that in mind because talented employees consider that too.

When I built my first machine learning program, an experienced database developer offered some advice. "You're great at using math and statistics," he said. "Definitely keep doing that. But whatever you do, don't let anyone put you in an analyst role. You can be way more talented than the developers, but you'll never make nearly as much money." He told me I should become a data scientist or a machine learning engineer to make sure I don't get underpaid.

Truth be told, I have no idea if he has facts to back that up. He also warned me against the "business intelligence developer" job title, but I've seen those roles make as much money as "database developers."

Regardless, the conversation stuck with me. I now always view calls from recruiters for "analyst" positions with skepticism.

Generalists versus Specialists

There are two broad categories for job roles in the data field: **generalists** and **specialists**.

Generalist job titles include:
1. Analyst
2. Business Intelligence Developer

Specialist job titles include:
1. Data Architect
2. Database Developer
3. Data Scientist
4. Data Strategist
5. Report Developer
6. Statistician

Many companies mistakenly assume you need more specialists as you hire more people. That works for some, but I have a better rule. Hire more specialists as the *volume* of work increases – not the size of the team.

Consider a team of three individuals receiving a handful of report requests per quarter and that also needs to build databases. This team should hire more generalists such as business intelligence developers. Since the team is small and the work is varied, this prevents one employee from roadblocking others when on vacation or working on another project. It's easier for each generalist to pick up on other people's work.

If the volume of report requests keeps one person busy every week, but you also need to develop new databases, then hire specialists, such as a database developer and a report developer.

Job Title: Analyst

"Analyst" is what employers call you when they don't know what else to call a data worker. Typically, analysts are entry-level positions. My first job title was analyst. Give this title to generalist roles without much technical experience and promote to BI Developer roles after gaining those skills. Analysts should be competent in spreadsheet tools like Excel or Google Sheets and have basic math skills at a bare minimum. Reporting tool experience is also good, but you can train them on tools if they don't have that experience.

Don't expect to attract high quality candidates with several years of experience with the analyst job title. You'll often see one analyst job posting to manipulate Excel workbooks and a different one to build complex reports and databases. With such a wide spectrum, quality candidates avoid this job title. In their eyes, the analyst title diminishes the perception of their skills.

When hiring analysts, look for:

- Less than one year experience in data
- Typically a recent college graduate
- Undergraduate degree in STEM, economics, or some other math-intensive major
- Great communication skills
- Curious and skeptical mindset

By the way, while I find STEM (science, technology, engineering, math) degrees are an easy way to filter down entry-level applicants, I've met many people with liberal arts backgrounds that also excel in data work. They're often much easier and more pleasant to work with as well.

Job Title: Business Intelligence Developer

This title attracts generalists with more experience. Typically, they're the jack-of-all trades and master of none. They may know Microsoft SSRS and SSIS, but wouldn't know how to use Python to build both an ETL process or reporting.

When hiring a BI developer, look for:

- A few years experience in ETL, reporting, and / or analysis
- Great communication skills

- Curious and skeptical mindset

Job Title: Data Architect

A data architect leads database developers when the volume and complexity of requests grow larger and needs a "master conductor" to manage workflow and increase efficiency. You only need to hire this role when volume reaches a certain tipping point though. Typically, a data architect leads requirements gathering for non-reporting projects, such as data warehouse development. They draw up detailed schemas and relationship diagrams for database developers to execute.

When hiring a data architect, look for:
- Several years of experience with database development
- Great leadership and communication abilities
- Great understanding of business strategy and principles

Job Title: Database Developer

A database developer takes requirements and builds or modifies a database to fulfill them. (Data engineer is another similar role that's growing in popularity.) They may take exact specifications from an architect or design the solution on their own. They must know SQL beyond simple SELECT * statements. They must be able to build databases, develop stored procedures, develop ETL processes to populate tables, and more.

When hiring a database developer, look for:
- Solid understanding of SQL or the ability to learn
- Solid understanding of ETL processes and technology
- Communication skills, if you expect them to directly gather requirements without a data architect's help
- Methodical approach to their work

Job Title: Data Scientist

Data Scientist is on the opposite end of the spectrum of an analyst. It's a catch-all title for when a company isn't sure what someone is supposed to do. They just want someone highly skilled at doing it.

I've asked multiple data workers what a data scientist does and I often get conflicting answers. My favorite definition is from Norman Niemer, Chief Data Scientist at UBS, who said, "A data scientist is a person who is better at statistics than any software engineer and better at software engineering than any statistician."

Nick Stevens, the Chief Data Officer at University of Kansas, gave a more descriptive answer. He said, "a data scientist to me focuses more on unstructured data and typically performs higher level analysis. [They] should have a very strong statistical background."

Sadly, data scientists often get roped into generalist activities to build data architecture, gather requirements, and help with basic reporting. Data scientists frequently switch jobs or are actively looking because role expectations frequently misalign with management requests.[8]

Generally, you should never have more data scientists than other roles. A highly skilled data scientist truly adds value only when you've already built your data architecture and satisfied basic reporting needs. Never try to skip the basics and leapfrog to machine learning, unless you're building ML-based software.

When hiring a data scientist, look for:

- A strong background in statistics (usually a masters degree)

[8] Brooks-Bartlett, J. (2018, April 17). Why so many data scientists are leaving their jobs. Retrieved July 28, 2020, from https://towardsdatascience.com/why-so-many-data-scientists-are-leaving-their-jobs-a1f0329d7ea4

- Expertise in statistical programming languages, such as R or Python
- Strong SQL skills
- Great communication skills, since they must frequently translate their work for less stats-savvy individuals

Job Title: Data Strategist

Data strategist is potentially a powerful role that delivers amazing solutions to stakeholders. A data strategist works with stakeholders, fosters consensus on their needs, and develops non-technical requirements for solutions.

Unfortunately most employers hire the wrong people for this role. There's an overemphasis on the *non-technical* part of the job description above. Employers tend to follow pop psychology, and they buy into the biggest myth that people are either "right brain" OR "left brain." They're creative OR they're analytical.

So they find a young "right brain" employee early in their career. Assuming that employee *only* thinks strategically and creatively. They're not expected to excel with technology because that's what "left brain" people do. These ambitious young employees typically want to become the "big picture" thinkers, so they take this opportunity when they're simply not ready.

That's a fundamental misunderstanding of how creativity works best though. Creativity works best when someone skilled at their trade applies the resources, knowledge, and techniques at their disposal in a new and innovative way. Because data strategists are often put in "big picture" roles before they really learn what technology can and cannot do, they don't actually deliver value.

For this role to actually add value, never treat it as an entry-level position. Promote tenured developers, architects, or data scientists into this role who show the ability to consider the big picture.

Don't believe me? Read the two examples below. The first is from Data Strategist A, without any development or data science experience. The other is from Data Strategist B, with such experience.

- Data Strategist A: "So it sounds like you want to know how many conversions you have on a monthly basis. Let me ask my developer if that's possible to do."
- Data Strategist B: "We can certainly report on conversions. We can even go further with higher level analysis. Would you like to know what combination of channels can maximize conversions?"

When hiring a data strategist, look for:

- Strong, practical experience in data or the industry you work in
- Solid understanding of what business intelligence and data science can do
- Great business sense
- Great communication skills

Job Title: Report Developer

A report developer (often called BI report developer or reporting analyst) takes data from a database and builds automated dashboards for stakeholders. They usually have a flare for design and consider how best to make data points easy to comprehend.

The best report developers know just enough SQL to write queries and build new data tables for reports. They know a reporting tool, such as SSRS, Domo, Tableau, or something similar. And they are great at requirements gathering.

Report development is a great proving ground for future data strategists, data scientists, and statisticians. Since reports are usually the destination for what database developers build, it's also a great place for natural data leaders to start their careers, since they will guide most of the requirements gathering discussions and need to communicate those requirements to other team members.

When hiring a report developer, look for:

- A curious and skeptical mindset
- Good business understanding
- Great communication skills (especially to lead meetings and stakeholder interviews)
- Great design skills
- Natural understanding of data and how it flows
- Decent SQL

Job Title: Statistician

The Statistician title is quickly being replaced by Data Scientist, but I think it's important and undervalued. Data scientists deal more with machine learning and unstructured data, applying statistics for predictive analytics. Statisticians, on the other hand, use statistics to find and understand the *relationships* between variables. Basically, statisticians are analysts on steroids.

Like data scientists, you shouldn't have too many statisticians, unless your data architecture is solid and you're more focused on analysis than development.

When hiring a statistician, look for:

- Programming skills in R, Python, SAS, or STATA
- A master's degree or multiple undergraduate courses in statistics (math majors have aptitude to learn statistics on their own)
- Academic research experience is helpful
- Great communication skills (you don't want them talking about p-values to stakeholders)

Things to Remember

- Data roles are either generalists or specialists
- Generalists are better investments for low-volume teams or companies
- Specialists are better investments for high-volume teams or companies

12

Best Personality Types for Data Work

Some personalities are perfect for data work. Others less so. After working with many different data workers, I notice certain types flourish while others fail spectacularly.

Truthfully, I always have sympathy for those who fail. They were likely attracted to data work because data science is "sexy," but they misunderstand what data work truly requires. They may not even know they're failing. Or they're unhappy and frustrated not knowing how to succeed in the field. With this chapter, I hope you can avoid hiring such people so they avoid a job they'll eventually hate.

I'm about to get more subjective than previous chapters, but keep the following info in mind if you're a manager or executive without much direct data experience. Maybe you were selected to lead a data team based on strong management experience, but you risk hiring or promoting the wrong people because of data inexperience.

I've found seven personality types or traits perfectly suited to data work:

1. Skeptics
2. Number Geeks
3. Tinkerers
4. Consensus Builders
5. Creatives

6. Storytellers
7. Life Learners

Don't expect to find someone with every trait though. These traits often determine what roles people take on as well and some are useless on their own. Storytellers, for example, are useless in data work if not combined with another trait like Math Geek.

In addition to the preferred traits, there's also seven key personalities unsuited to data work:
1. Know-it-alls
2. Bossypants
3. Blamers
4. Reactionaries
5. Incurious
6. Technically Averse
7. Rogues

People to Hire and Retain in Data Work

Skeptics

Skeptics are the best people to hire for data work. They're never satisfied with surface-level answers. During a job interview, they'll ask, "So how does that actually work? Don't you ever have an issue with such-and-such happening?"

It's not that they *need* to be convinced, but that they *want* to be convinced. They want facts, often remaining unsure of personal assumptions until proved right with objective evidence.

Skeptics are actually easy to spot at your company. They're often subject matter experts telling you what's wrong with your data. They know the data better than you ever will. They'll pull up a source tool and show you exact discrepancies. These have always been my favorite subject matter experts by the way.

I once worked with an SEO specialist. I sometimes discussed reporting with her, and she'd open a dashboard and compare it to website tracking in Google Analytics. She pointed out exact discrepancies. I told her she should work in business intelligence. She said no thanks.

Math Geeks

Math Geeks major in math, economics, physics, or another STEM degree in college. I don't think I've ever met someone great at math and terrible at data work (although I've certainly met some with bad attitudes). Math Geeks are easier to hire since their degrees directly reflect those skills. If you ever need to hire an entry-level person in a hurry, a STEM degree quickly narrows down aptitude to learn data work.

Learning to read mathematical notations prepares you to learn how to code. Mathematical notations often describe what's happening to data, only a computer isn't showing you the results. Whenever you start doing calculus, you imagine what the equation does to the inputted data.

Another benefit, Math Geeks intuitively think about how to apply upper-level statistics to solving problems. While few use multiple linear regressions on a daily basis, standard deviation and measures of variance have very powerful and underused applications in data work. It's far more challenging to train math-averse people in these methods than simply hiring Math Geeks who already know how.

I suggest hiring at least one Math Geek for your team.

Tinkerers

Tinkerers are cousins to Math Geeks. You'll seldom find a Tinkerer and Math Geek rolled into one though. If you do, they'll be expensive to hire. They probably fix their own refrigerator or their own car when either breaks down. They REALLY fell in love with programming, maybe in their early teens or late twenties.

Once they started, they kept digging deeper and deeper into the technology.

Tinkerers love learning out new tips and tricks with every new software release. They live for "light bulb" moments on how best to apply a new feature.

Ideally, you want at least one Tinkerer on your team and one Math Geek. Their collaboration produces amazing results. For example, I'm more of a Math Geek. I've only used programming to the extent my job requires. At a previous job, I worked with a bonafide Tinkerer. He understood statistics, but didn't have the same drive I did for using it.

Trying to build an algorithm, I explained to him I needed to calculate the impact of categorical variables on the output on a massive scale. After some pondering, he had a "light bulb" moment. He remembered an old research article he saved on Bayesian networks. He didn't fully understand what the math entailed, but he assisted a colleague at a previous job with the related programming. Together, we built the first machine learning program and uncovered over $100k in missing revenue for our employer!

Consensus Builders

Consensus building is the most underrated skill for data workers. Just to get hired, I think they need to be Math Geeks or Tinkerers, but long-term success depends on their ability to build consensus. Projects typically have multiple stakeholders with competing viewpoints. Data workers simply can't wait for one of them to proactively write a requirements document. They must step forward, lead meetings, and guide stakeholders to consensus.

If you don't have at least one team member good at this, your data solutions are doomed to fail.

Identifying Consensus Builders in interviews is hard, but you can easily spot them inside your company. When setting up a meeting, they always include an agenda and a list of must-have decisions for an effective meeting outcome. During the meeting, they ask opinions of quieter colleagues with relevant expertise. They play devil's advocate, bringing up counterpoints. All these activities serve the greater purpose of developing the best solution for *all* stakeholders.

Creatives

Creatives are full of ideas. Positively brimming over. While I suspect many workplaces hire too many thinkers and not enough doers, you still need a few Creatives on your team. They innovate and think up solutions no one even considered before. They have light bulb moments mid-meeting and also the confidence to pitch it on the spot.

I still recommend a strong foundation in math or technology, so they know what *will* or *should* work and not go wild with unfeasible ideas.

Storytellers

Storytellers deliver insights in an easy-to-understand way and design reports that end users can easily digest. There's an annoying analytics cliche: "We tell a story with the data." But it's so common for good reason – stakeholders want it. Succeeding here goes a long way.

A good Storyteller takes complex material and simplifies for a general audience. Instead of building data dump PowerPoints, they think through how to use data, visual aids, and verbal communication to engage the audience. Instead of building jam-packed dashboards, they scale back and focus on business questions.

I've always focused on this area myself. In my senior year of college, my economics professor was reviewing econometric concepts. He pointed to something on the marker board called the beta coefficient. He asked me what it meant. I said, "Beta coefficient is 32." He stared blankly and said, "I asked you what it meant. Not what it was." He wanted a data story, not a factual observation.

The lesson: your audience typically doesn't care how you conducted the analysis. They want insights and recommendations.

Life Learners

Life Learners is something Jared Sloan, Vice President of Data Solutions at Alight Analytics, told me to include in this chapter. I like him, so I did.

Life Learners are hard to find, but once you do, work hard to retain them. They may have several past jobs. They're constantly reading or taking a Python class during their spare time, even though the job doesn't require Python. Tinkerers often share this trait as well since they have a natural affinity for new technologies.

Life Learners who aren't coders are usually strong candidates to groom and promote to leadership positions. Data strategist is a good role for them too.

People to NOT Hire in Data Work

Know-it-alls

Know-it-alls are the worst to hire in data work. They're experts without expertise. They're quite sure they know enough already and don't need stakeholder input. They're the antithesis of the Skeptic. Skeptics want to be convinced, while Know-it-alls immediately start trying to convince you.

This is a bad quality (and not just an annoying quirk) because it's so easy to be proven wrong in data work. Someone who speaks confidently without checking facts first has a tendency to damage credibility quickly. Since your employee's behavior reflects your overall team, this negative impact amplifies.

Bossypants

Bossypants (to borrow my niece's favorite insult) have trouble keeping leadership abilities in check. They're delegators without actual authority to delegate. They tell colleagues what to do and berate them (or tattle to the boss) if those colleagues don't follow orders.

This trait kills team morale and muddies management roles and responsibilities on the team. Redirect people who assert their way of doing things on others to specific roles, such as training or onboarding, where such behavior is actually beneficial. That scratches their itch to influence others and also saves more experienced employees the indignity of constantly being told what to do by Bossypants colleagues.

Blamers

Blamers are always innocent. They do everything right and everyone else (management, stakeholders, and "the man") are in the wrong. They're perpetually set up to fail, especially that project they said would be done four weeks ago that they never even started. Blamers, in other words, are self-styled victims.

Blamers have a point...sometimes. Maybe management (you) didn't build a process or system empowering them to succeed, but there's a limit. I find Blamers often don't have the technical or emotional skills needed to succeed in data work and deflect by pointing out what's wrong with other people.

Reactionaries

Reactionaries are usually insecure and afraid of looking like failures. When something doesn't map correctly in the data, they add a CASE statement as a "quick fix." Reactionaries make too many quick fixes though, degrading system quality over time.

Reactionaries are mostly well-intentioned. They want to serve the stakeholder well. Other times they're deflecting blame or criticism. They look like a problem solver, but they're really just burying the problem to resurface later.

Early career professionals commonly fall into this trap. Young, smart workers want to look dependable. That includes me. I also patched data issues with hacky fixes early in my data work career. I've learned the shortsightedness of this approach over time though.

Coach Reactionaries to improve communication skills and keep insecurities in check. They must have tough conversations with stakeholders about the importance of long-term fixes over short-term patches. Short-term patches eventually wear thin and fail, making it worse for the stakeholder in the long run.

Incurious

Usually the best data workers are self-proclaimed nerds. They want to learn everything. A new coding language? Yes please. A random fact about demographic trends? Tell me more. Their ears naturally perk whenever they're about to learn something new.

People who lack curiosity are not well suited to data work. You need natural curiosity about business strategies when you walk into stakeholder interviews. You naturally want to ask, "Why is that important to you?" or "What does a successful brand awareness campaign look like to you?"

Without curiosity, you won't truly understand the problems you're solving and the data you're building solutions with.

Technically Averse

I've met people with data science degrees who avoid SQL and math. As I said before, you must have a strong foundation in at least one of them to be a data worker. Some try to circumvent this by aiming straight for data strategy roles, but I think data strategy is best reserved for creative thinkers with intensive programming or math experience.

Rogues

No one wants anarchists managing their data. You might be the best developer, mathematician, and storyteller in the world, but if your solutions do not follow company best practices and integrate seamlessly with established system architecture, your work output can have a net negative impact.

Good developers usually disagree with one another, but understand the importance of consistency. If they prefer certain coding best practices or naming conventions, they deliberate and vote on the matter. They know conforming to a "good enough" standardized plan is better than each individual developer doing what they think is best.

Things to Remember

- Every data worker needs to be a Math Geek or Tinkerer or both
- Successful data workers are typically natural Skeptics as well
- Consensus Builder, Creative, Storyteller, and Life Learner traits set up data workers for long-term success